Noah

Flying Eagle Publications

We aspire to create materials that encourage and strengthen you in your journey through life. It is also our aim to equip believers so that they can reach farther dream larger and get their message heard. The eagle flies closest to the Creator and bears His message to all. That is our hope too. That is why we do what we do— to teach, entertain and inspire.

Noah

Flying Eagle Publications

Unless otherwise noted, all scripture taken from the King James Version of the Bible. Scriptures marked KJV are taken from the KING JAMES VERSION (KJV): KING JAMES VERSION, public domain.

Scriptures marked CEV are taken from the CONTEMPORARY ENGLISH VERSION (CEV):Scripture taken from the CONTEMPORARY ENGLISH VERSION copyright© 1995 by the American Bible Society. Used by permission.

Noah
ISBN: 978 1 7327688-0-2

Copyright ©Flying Eagle Publications 2018. Cover image courtesy of Canva.
All Rights Reserved under International Copyright Law. No part of this book may be reproduced or transmitted in any form or by any means.
 Flyingeaglepublications.com

Printed in the United States

*T*he little book you hold in your hands is a journey. You are following the path of Noah's story. We, the writers, are serving as guides, pointing out items of interest along the way. It is not a complete history. Each bit of news is like the limb on a tree. You can trace it to its end or discover new trails along twisting branches, study each leaf and admire the fruit of truth in your sleuthing.

The purpose of this writing is to show you the story of Noah is far from fable. It is to fortify confidence in the WORD, and reveal the noisy barking of a large, toothless black dog called Evolution. It is to right wrongs, the misconceptions swirling around truth, hoping to drown it in a whirlpool of ignorance and modernity.

But before we begin our study of Noah, we need to learn about the two kinds of knowledge: sense knowledge and revelation knowledge.

Sense knowledge is the way most education comes to us, through sight, smell, touch, taste and sound. Our five senses are the tools we use to transfer information to our mind. Our mind reasons. Knowledge comes as we reflect and study. Sense knowledge limits itself to what can be observed.

Therefore this type of knowledge is limited. It can only proceed as far as the capacity to take in what is available to the senses. It depends on the mind to interpret the information correctly. This type of knowledge can be unreliable and may need to be updated or revised.

Revelation knowledge comes to us through God's word. *Webster's 1828 American Dictionary of the English Language* defines *revelation* as "The act of disclosing or discovering to others what was before unknown to them." Revelation is telling. It is given. We do not have to search out, wonder, guess or try to solve puzzles. It is truth revealed. It may come to us through seeing or hearing (in the case of the blind, touching) but it is not gained by human wisdom.

Paul contrasts the two types of knowledge in 1 Corinthians 1:22-23 when he teaches about knowing God. "For since in the wisdom of God the world by wisdom did not know God, God was pleased through the foolishness of preaching to save the ones believing. And since Jews ask for a sign, and Greeks seek wisdom." (YLT)

The world's wisdom is sense knowledge; it comes through the flesh, asking for signs to observe or seeking wisdom in other places than God's word.

These two types of knowledge will be on display throughout the following chapters. As men have rejected God's word as a source of reliable information, sense knowledge is all that is left to them. It limits, hinders and drives them in circles, always learning but never coming to the truth.

Others, scientists, historians, professionals and blue collars included, have welcomed revelation knowledge. For example, from Marshall Hall the physiologist to George Washington Carver to Peter J. Daniels and Ben Carson, all respected in their field in their generation, they have invited God into their work for the good of mankind.

Sense knowledge has overtaken the church because we've been steeped in the education of our culture for a long time. Evolution is sense knowledge, and it has changed the way we view the Bible. But the Bible stands. Still revealing truth.

Another aspect of interpreting facts is worldview, what you believe to be true and your understanding of how the world works. Everyone has one. It is what we use to determine our values and goals. Governments are founded upon them, and families and educational systems operate from them.

This book is written from an uncompromised biblical worldview, meaning we do not believe in mixing another worldview with what the Bible claims to be true. A biblical worldview accepts the Bible as truth. There are other worldviews that claim to be neutral, but there is no neutral. The Bible is believed or it is not. It cannot be divided into sections like Partly Reliable, Not Sure, Reliable, Not Reliable. The reason is because the Author is God. He is not a man that lies. He is Truth. And, He is kind enough to reveal His wisdom to us so we do not have to grope for answers.

Speaking of groping for answers, we've offered simple pronunciation guides in parentheses for most difficult foreign words. But there are some that are ancient and unknown or have various pronunciations or can be deciphered by basic English phonetics. These you are welcome to grapple with like the rest of us.

We pray you enjoy your journey and that it opens the way to deeper meditation on Noah, his story and what it means to us today.

~*The Editors*

• Chapter 1 •

What Noah Knew

In the beginning. With these three words the mystery of origins unfolds. There is the mystery of the earth and the vast heavens above it; the mystery of all that flies, creeps, crawls, walks, swims and glides; the mystery of all that grows and multiplies, and especially the mystery of us.

Questions fill our heads. How did all these things come about? And why? What is the reason for it all? Why am I different from every other animal on earth?

Three words introduce the answers to our questions. Genesis is the first book of the Bible. Moses wrote it while traveling around in the desert wilderness of Saudi Arabia. But Moses lived over 2,000 years after Adam. How did Moses know what to write?

There are many myths about ancient man. Let's find out what Noah knew about the first men.

Man Could Speak

The first thing we need to understand is that man was created speaking a language right away. On the day God made Adam, they were speaking to each other, and Adam was naming animals. Gen 2:19 says, "And out of the ground the LORD God formed every beast of the field, and every fowl of the air; and brought them unto Adam to see what he would call them: and whatsoever Adam called every living creature, that was the name thereof."

God talked with Adam. He showed Adam his need for a helper and friend. He told him how to take care of the earth, and He visited with Adam and Eve in the garden. Many science and history books are written by people who do not believe this about early man. They believe man had to discover how to speak to one another, how to write, how to make clothes, gather food, hunt, farm and so on. But the Bible shows us that God taught them the plants they could eat, and He even made clothes for them. "Unto Adam also and to his wife did the LORD God make coats of skins, and clothed them." (Genesis 3:21)

In fact, archaeologists are finding that the earliest people did have complex languages and were able to write. In eastern China experts discovered a language they say is 5,000 years old. Complex means the language uses words that can be arranged and connected to create meaning. It uses words in sentences not symbols to tell a story. The inscription shows six Chinese characters in a line.

Even using pictographs, there is no evidence of simple languages in the history of ancient man as in the idea of a grunting caveman. Whenever a new people group was found, evolutionists hoped it would prove their theory simple languages grew more complex with time. But no such progression was found. Instead, the language principle demonstrates the exact opposite. It proves all living languages, the languages spoken today, are changing and becoming more simple.[1]

For an example, compare the King James Bible and the Contemporary English Version using John 3:20.

---

[1] Laurie J. White. *King Alfred's English*, "Chapter 3 A Little About English."

"For every one that doeth evil hateth the light, neither cometh to the light, lest his deeds should be reproved." KJV

"People who do evil hate the light and won't come to the light, because it clearly shows what they have done." CEV

Someday the easier version will have to be updated again so people will understand the meaning of words they find difficult. The language principle shows there is an evolution of the language. But it is being dumbed down, the term used in many articles on the subject.

One question evolutionists find hard to answer is if man lived for billions of years, why did it take him so long to learn to speak, read and write? Why do written languages only go back to 5,000 years or so? Why the sudden surge of intelligence?

Think of what man has invented in the last two hundred years. We are pretty smart, but we still can't figure out some of ancient man's inventions like Greek fire.[2] We also are surprised to find 2,000 year old batteries, earthquake detectors, Greek computers, light bulbs sketched into Egyptian art, or pyramids and other structures built without heavy equipment.

The truth is there was no such surge. The records go back to around 5,000 years because that is when they started keeping records again, after the flood. Languages are about 5,000 years old because that is the age men began multiplying again, after the flood.

The Bible shows us God was speaking before He created Adam. He used words to communicate His will and as the means for His creative power. According to Jewish tradition, the language God used to speak with Adam was Hebrew. We cannot prove that, but some creationists and Christian scholars favor this view because the list of Adam's descendants is Hebrew names. Is it possible God spoke Hebrew to create the world? What do you think? One

---

[2] A flaming weapon used in naval battles that continued to burn on water.

thing the Bible makes clear is that all the people spoke one language before the flood. Language study hints that language was advanced.

Man Could Write

When Moses wrote Genesis, he wrote using Hebrew oral and written records as his guide. This was thought to be impossible. The oldest book in the Bible is Job. In it Job says, "Oh that my words were now written! oh that they were printed in a book! That they were graven with an iron pen and lead in the rock for ever!" (Job 19:23-24) Apparently he got his wish. Job's story was written down because we are reading it today.

Archaeological discoveries near the Sinai Desert's ancient turquoise mines show inscriptions at Serabit el-Khadim. They seem to be written by common laborers, probably slaves. This find shatters the idea that only scribes or educated people could write. Abraham, the ancestor of the Jewish people, lived in Ur, the richest city in the land. Even the common district had schools and libraries, and the people were wealthy. If the first "Hebrew" person was likely to read and write, why not his descendants?

Isaiah calls the Hebrew language the language of Canaan. "In that day shall five cities in the land of Egypt speak the language of Canaan, and swear to the LORD of hosts..." Historians and linguists think the Sumerian language is the oldest language and predates the flood. They have always claimed the Phoenician alphabet was the original alphabet. Using these ideas as their base to make more decisions, they thought Hebrew as well as other languages developed from the Sumerian and Phoenician languages. The word Semite comes from the Hebrew Shem. Semitic languages are those related to Shem's children of which Sumerian and Phoenician belong. *Fox News, Science News* and others, however, report a recent discovery by Professor Douglas Petrovich. The oldest known alphabet is Hebrew.

Petrovich's discovery is not new. In the early 1900s, findings such as the inscriptions at Serabit el-Khadim were referred to as Proto Sinaitic, Proto Canaanite or Paleo Hebrew. This shows Hebrew was already being identified as an ancient alphabet. Other researchers, including W.F. Albright and Hubert Grimme have identified the Serabit el-Khadim alphabet as Semitic/Hebrew.

In studying these inscriptions and more, Professor Petrovich confirmed their theories. So we can be confident that Hebrews had an alphabet and could write in their own language or were educated to use another. They were fully capable of communicating their early history to each other and recording it.

The Hebrew people also had a system of repetition and storytelling tradition. First a general outline was given. Then more details were added. The system made it possible to keep accurate records. This trait is seen in archaeological discoveries like the Dead Sea Scrolls, the Copper Scrolls, the Silver Amulets and many other steles and monuments. Their historical accounts have proven accurate, even listing the flaws and mistakes of their leaders.

We said that Moses used Hebrew oral and written sources to write the history of creation. You may wonder how we know. Genesis 2:4 says, "These are the generations of the heaven and the earth when they were created." *Towlĕdah* (toe-lay-DOTH) is the Hebrew word we translate as generations, and it means history or origin. Moses was saying, "This is the history," and his readers knew he was quoting from the record. Moses used the same words many times in Genesis as an introduction to another section of history.

For example, here are other places in Genesis where the word is used: Genesis 5:1; 6:9; 10:1; 10:32; 11:10; 11:27; 25:12-13 and 19; 36:1 and 9; 37:2.

The practice of keeping family records might seem far-fetched, but archaeology discovered the practice when the Nuzi Tablets were found. Nuzi was a city close to the Hurrian capital of Kirkuk in Iraq. The Hurrians are the Horites, Hivites and Jebusites of the Bible.

The Nuzi Tablets revealed over 5,000 family and government records. It showed family records were highly honored and kept, being passed down, father to son, for six generations. Dr. Bryant G. Wood states:

> "Nowhere else in the ancient Near East is this kind of reverence for family documents illustrated, except in the Old Testament. Indirectly, the practice at Nuzi supports the position that Genesis and the other books of history in the Old Testament are grounded in actual family, clan and tribal records carefully passed from generation to generation."[3]

Mankind Lived Long Lives

Something else Noah knew was that early man lived for hundreds of years. Adam died only two hundred years before Noah was born. Noah's father knew him. Adam's son Seth lived at the same time Noah was a young man. Noah's son Shem was still living when Abraham was traveling in Canaan. Eber (AY-vare) is considered by most to be the origin of the word Hebrew. He was a great grandson of Shem and lived to be 464 years old. He was still alive when Abraham died. Abraham's grandson, Jacob (Israel), was fifty when Shem died. Jacob was seventy nine when Eber died.

Can you see how easily the stories could be kept? If someone tried to make up a story, there was someone, an eyewitness, who could tell the truth. Lies could be uncovered quickly.

Man Was Created

Genesis 1 and 2 tell us how God created the world. Man is the only creation He made in His image. Man is also the only creation God breathed His DNA into, and the only one He gave dominion over the rest of creation. Man-

---

[3]Bryant G. Wood. "Great Discoveries in Biblical Archaeology: The Nuzi Tablets." AFBR.

kind, man and woman, were to rule over the rest. That is why man is not equal to animals. He rules over them and has a special place of fellowship with God the Creator. Evolution brings us down to the level of animals. That is what Satan would like us to believe about ourselves today because it lowers our place of authority on the earth. But man is a spirit being, like God.

Mankind was made a little lower than Elohim. "For thou hast made him a little lower than the angels, and hast crowned him with glory and honour." (Psalms 8:5) The word translated angels is *elohim*. *Young's Literal Translation of the Bible* says, "And causest him to lack a little of Godhead, And with honour and majesty compassest him." God chose man as a companion and encircled him, ʿatar (uh-TARE), in glory. Some believe Adam was first clothed with glory in the form of light.

Since Adam was created on the sixth day, we might wonder how he knew what happened on days one through six. How would he know about the beginning of the earth, the sun, moon and stars, the plants and animals? The answer is simple: 1. God told him. 2. He was created with age, not born a baby.

Whether Adam asked first or God described what He had done as He showed Adam around the garden doesn't matter. God wanted us to know. The history was written so we would know the story of our beginning and the supreme power and ability of God. Creation, including us, is a reminder of a God who is bigger, smarter and more powerful than we are. There is nothing impossible for Him. God created the earth in six days in a way that defied what we know of science. Isn't it amazing what God could do in one day?

And it was one day. The Hebrew record keepers made sure we understood that by using their word *yom* with the words evening and morning. It is on purpose they add first day, second day, etc. Hugh Williamson, Emanuel Tov and other Hebrew scholars recognize the effort made to eliminate any doubts. [4]

---

[4] Jud Davis. "24 Hours—Plain as Day." *Answers Magazine*.

If the meaning is plain to those who are experts in the Hebrew language, then it is also plain that you have to go outside the Bible to claim the world was created in billions of years. The Bible does not support an old earth. There are many scientists who say science doesn't either.

Later in the Bible, the word day is a symbol for one thousand years. (Psalm 90:4, Hosea 6:2, 2Peter 3:3-4,8) Hosea and Peter are speaking of the last days as Peter calls them. The Hebrews believed mankind would have about 6,000 years of history before Jesus came again, and their verses are talking about that. But in the first chapter of Genesis, with the addition of morning and evening, the words make it clear it was a day like the ones we know.

Genesis 2 gives us more detail than Genesis 1. This is an example of the Hebrew storytelling method. First they give the general story; then they fill in with details. Genesis 2:5-6 says a mist came from the ground every night to water the plants and trees. A river flowed through the land and also provided water. This river separated into four rivers. These rivers are the Tigris, Euphrates, Pishon and Gihon. The land of Havilah had gold and precious gems. Today there is a place called Havilah located in the Arabian Penninsula near the Persian Gulf. The land of Cush is called Ethiopia today.

This region of the four rivers was where the Garden of Eden was. The Bible says the Garden was in Eden, making Eden a region. The exact location of Eden is not known. But scholars like to guess anyway. They use satellite imaging to find ancient riverbeds and study ancient writings. Some locate it at the head of the Tigris and Euphrates near Turkey and Iraq. Others put it where the rivers flow into the Persian Gulf. Still others say east of the Nile which they claim is the Pishon, north of Arabia and east of Iran.

One thing to remember is that we don't even know if the Tigris and Euphrates Rivers after the flood are the original Tigris and Euphrates before the flood. For instance, there are places in America named in honor of other towns settlers knew like New York, New Amsterdam, Philadelphia, Cairo, Athens, Lima, New Madrid, etc. *Eshkani-ziibi* is the Anishinaabe name for a river in Ontario, Canada. It means horned or antlered river in the Odawa and Ojibwe languages. In 1793, Lieutenant Governor John Graves Simcoe named it the Thames after the River Thames in London.

From these examples we learn it is possible the Tigris and Euphrates were named for those Noah and his sons had known before. Both rivers begin in the Armenian Highlands in eastern Turkey near Mt. Ararat. The landscape had changed drastically after the flood and perhaps the rivers as well because they run on top of rock buried by the deluge. And that is most likely where the Garden of Eden is, buried under rock somewhere.

Even though we don't know exactly where the original Garden is, we may know where it is not. Genesis 2:13-14 mentions Ethiopia and Assyria. Moses is the writer, inspired by the Holy Spirit who knows where the Garden was. And, Moses knew the names used in his day for the regions he wanted to indicate. It is possible Moses wrote the information in locations his readers would recognize. If so, we have a general idea that seems to include Israel's boundaries and we can rule out places like Motuo, Tibet or Socotra Island.

Mankind had a wonderful beginning. Like a doting parent, God made a home perfectly decked out for his children. Everything had a purpose. The plants, animals, seas, sun moon and stars, all that was seen and unseen were for man's enjoyment and existence on earth.

Man Betrayed God

The first chapters of Genesis do not give us detailed information of all of Adam's children. It does not name his other sons and daughters in Genesis 5:4, "And the days of Adam after he had begotten Seth were eight hundred years: and he begat sons and daughters," or tell us about their sons and daughters.

It was written as a history for the Jewish people and focused on their line of ancestors.

It does tell us about Cain. Cain had a bad attitude about bringing sacrifices to God. He did not do what was best. It made him angry when God accepted his brother Abel's sacrifice and not his. When God spoke to him about changing his attitude, Cain became angry. He did not want to change his behavior or his attitude. He killed Abel and then had to leave the place where his father and other brothers and sisters were living.

How could Cain become so cruel and do such things? God had created a beautiful world. But that world was very different from the one we know today. For instance, all animals ate seeds and plants and never fought with each other. Some even talked.

We don't know for sure when it happened, but a war broke out among the heavenly host which included angels. One of these beings named Lucifer wanted to be like God. Of course no one can be as powerful or as wise as God, since we are created by Him. We cannot create men or worlds like God did. We can only continue what He established. The angels are also created beings. But Lucifer wanted what he wanted no matter how foolish it was.

He persuaded one third of the angels to fight with him against God, but they lost. No longer part of the heavenly angels, Lucifer roamed between earth and heaven, jealous of this new creature God had made in His image called man. God had given the rule of the whole earth to this pitiful human who was no where near as magnificent a being as an angel, he thought. What if he, Lucifer, could trick this man into giving him the rule of the earth and everything in it?

He made a plan to do just that. He knew God had given this Adam free will. He had one too. It meant he and Adam could make their own choices. All Lucifer had to do was to get Adam to choose him over God.

But he had no right to be in the garden. Adam was the boss there. He needed to be crafty. Lucifer took on the form of a reptile and waited for Eve and her Adam to show up. When they did, he started talking:

"And he said to the woman, 'Is it so that God has said, You shall not eat of every tree of the garden?' And the woman said to the serpent, 'We may eat of the fruit of the trees of the garden. But of the fruit of the tree which is in the middle of the garden, God has said, You shall not eat of it, neither shall you touch it, lest you die.' And the serpent said to the woman, 'You shall not surely die, for God knows that in the day you eat of it, then your eyes shall be opened, and you shall be as God, knowing good and evil.' " (Genesis 3:1-5)

To be like God was what Lucifer wanted. Adam and Eve already were like God. They also knew about good. What they didn't know about was evil and all that it brought: pain, sickness, sorrow and death. If you would have told Adam about a sore throat or that you can feel sick, he would not have known what you meant. He had never experienced sickness or pain.

God did know about evil and didn't want mankind to experience it. He told them not to eat of that tree for their own good. By obeying Him, they would have defeated Lucifer and become very wise. The Bible says respecting and honoring God brings wisdom. (Proverbs 9:10)

Adam knew the commands God had given him. He understood his authority over the animals, including a wayward reptile. Some debate whether Adam heard Lucifer's words. They think Eve talked with Lucifer first and later when she was with Adam persuaded him to eat it. Romantics and poets like Milton say Adam ate because he loved Eve and didn't want to be without her. Jewish tradition says Adam heard the whole thing. Either way, Adam made a decision to disobey God.

The Bible does not say Adam was deceived. He allowed Eve's deception and allowed her to eat first. Romans 5 speaks of Adam's sin not Eve's. Neither one trusted God, however. Instead they trusted their judgment, believed Lucifer, and he became their master. Adam did not realize the consequence of his decision, that Lucifer would take away his dominion. Lucifer kept that a secret. But, Adam found out quickly because Lucifer wanted the rule of the earth. And, as Adam and Eve discovered, his ways are opposite of all God's ways.

The Result of Man's Betrayal

Since Adam and Eve lost their right to rule, they had to leave the Garden. God told Adam under Lucifer's rule life would not be easy. His life became hard, and all the earth was affected.

When Cain committed his horrible crime, Adam may have remembered the day of his own sin and how he had to leave the garden God had made for him. It must have grieved him that it was his fault this angel's rebellion had taken over earth.

It is sad man disobeyed God so quickly. But Adam and Eve told their story and Cain's story anyway. Why do you think Adam wanted us to know this sad history? Do you think God wanted us to know it?

It is important early man kept records. God wanted these things written so we who live six thousand years later would know our Creator and how the earth and all it contains came to be. Romans 1:20 says, "For the invisible things of him [God] from the creation of the world are clearly seen, being understood by the things that are made, even his eternal power and Godhead."

He also wanted us to know our place in the world. God wanted us to know how special we are out of all His creation, that we are the only beings created in His likeness, a spirit being. He gave us the ability to make decisions, and like He did with Adam and Eve, He desires to talk to us.

An important fact to remember is man is not on the level of an animal. God wanted us to know that He has always wanted to be our friend and good Father, and that He desires and is able to provide for our every need. Adam had a good life before Lucifer tempted him to reject God's ways. It was Lucifer who lowered mankind in rank. He continues to work at it, now trying to make him an animal or make him doubt God.

God also wanted us to know how Eve was tricked by words, how Lucifer twisted what God had said and got her thinking in a way that seemed right to her. Adam and Eve's disobedience brought sin and death into God's perfect world. Today, when people disobey God and bad things happen, we can know that God never wanted the earth to be like this. He never wanted people to choose to disobey. But He gave them freedom. That freedom included the ability to make choices. God has never changed His mind, but He allows and honors mankind's right to choose.

It is hard for us to realize how much sin influences our world. It can be seen in nature when animals kill each other, in harsh weather and disasters. It is the cause of disease in every living thing, of hatred and death. It is the cause of people being poor and starving.

There are people who have had glimpses of heaven. One thing they tell us is the beauty of the colors there. That is because there is a veil of darkness in the earth because of sin. The Bible tells us there is no darkness in God. His pure light exists in heaven because there is no sin there. It is hard to imagine a cloud of pollution hanging over the earth because of sin, but that is what it is like.

Lucifer assured Eve that if she ate the fruit she would not die. Of course he lied. There were two deaths Adam and Eve suffered. First was the death of their spirit connection to God. They still had a spirit, but disobedience separated them from God. The second death was physical. It would be some time before they experienced physical death.

God's Promise

God told Adam and Eve that one day out of Eve would come a Deliverer who could undo the bad things they had brought upon the earth and into the heart of man. God wanted to provide this Deliverer because He is love. Adam believed God, and he gave Eve her name. Eve means the mother of all the living. Whoever this Deliverer would be, they would restore man's place above the serpent, Lucifer.

This was what Noah knew. He and his family and all of his neighbors were speaking one complex language. In that language, Noah heard the story of creation, how mankind became evil and how the world was changed. He lived in this changed world and raised a family. He chose to follow God. He also heard the story of the promised Deliverer.

We know the Deliverer God spoke of was Jesus. We know His mother's name was Mary, and she defeated Lucifer by her words. She said to the angel Gabriel, "...be it unto me according to thy word." So with words man's downfall began, and with words man's salvation began.

Jesus came 4000 years after Adam. Around 2,000 after Noah. He came to live a perfect life and die on the cross, taking all the sin people had done or would do upon Himself. He volunteered to be punished for all mankind so they could be forgiven by God. When He did this, He defeated Lucifer's rule. Jesus provided a way of escape for us so we can live a blessed life now on earth and be with Jesus forever. What many do not realize is He restored our dominion and authority. (Ephesians 1 and 2)

He truly is a Deliverer for those who want Him, but it is our choice to accept this forgiveness or not. If we do not, we are living under Lucifer's government. We will have to pay the penalty for the bad things we do just like our master Lucifer. The Hebrew word to describe Lucifer is *satan* (suh-TAN). It means adversary or one who works against us. Satan is man's enemy.

Many refuse the gift Jesus offers us. But God hopes we will take His gift. We call this gift salvation because it saves us from punishment and all the bad things Satan can do to us.

The question we have to answer is, what will we do with our free will? Who will we choose to be our master, Satan or Jesus?

So there is the story of our beginnings. God gives us the choice to believe it or not. Noah believed. Noah chose to obey, and it saved his life.

• Chapter 2 •

Noah's World

Creation was the beginning of mankind as we know him. There are teachers of the Bible who think millions of years are wrapped up in the creation of the world. They point to Genesis 1:1-2 and say a gap of time is between the verses. They think dinosaurs lived in these gap years for thousands of years. Some think men lived in this gap too.

A prophet named Jeremiah once had a vision of our ancient earth while seeing the destruction of Israel. (Jeremiah 4:23-26) He said, "I beheld the earth, and, lo, it was without form, and void; and the heavens, and they had no light." This was a condition only mentioned in Genesis 1:2. The gap teachers point to Jeremiah's words as proof of their idea. But Jeremiah saw the earth *destroyed*. That is just how we find the earth in Genesis 1:2. Without form. Nothing on it. Then, no dinosaur tracks or bones from the gap days would be seen on our earth. If we see fossils and bones of animals today, they are from the earth created in Genesis 1:3 onward.

There are others who believe this gap and Jeremiah's vision tell us when Satan rebelled against God. The word *hâyâh* (hi-YAH) is translated was in Genesis 1:2. "And the earth [*hâyâh*] was without form, and void..." It means happen, come to pass and became. The second *was* in the verse is inserted for English grammar. "...and darkness *was* upon the face of the deep." But the first was is really in the sense of it became. The earth became formless and void. To some this is significant because it is the same word used for God's creative power in Genesis 1:3. "Let there be [*hâyâh*] light." To others it represents the Hebrew storytelling method. God made the earth and then He molded it.

The gap theory and Jeremiah's prophecy aside, it is possible there was an age before ours. Revelation says God will make a new earth and a new heaven. "And I saw a new heaven and a new earth: for the first heaven and the first earth were passed away; and there was no more sea." (Revelation 21:1) If He is going to destroy and create earth again, He could have done it before.

The Bible also mentions future ages. "That in the ages to come he might shew the exceeding riches of his grace in his kindness toward us through Christ Jesus." Perhaps like a sculptor remolding his clay, God will take us on grand adventures as He creates new earth ages. Then we will have a front row seat much like the angels do in our time. Only better because God says we get to reign and rule with Him.

But the only age we know for certain is ours. Revelation tells how our age will end, and it gives us a glimpse of our future life. It will be wonderful! Revelation also tells about a new beginning for us. We don't know all of it. How could we? We are still learning about our beginning on earth!

In 1654, Archbishop James Ussher dated the creation of the world to October 22 or 23, 4004 BC. He used the Julian calendar. A second century rabbi named Jose ben Halafta figured 3761 BC was the day God created the world. Scientists like Johannes Kepler, Sir Isaac Newton and others tried to find the year too. They all agreed that creation happened around four thousand BC, give or take a few years. It may be harder to pinpoint the exact day, though Jewish tradition does say it happened on Rosh Hashanah.

Could Ussher be right about the year? Well, using his sources, he dated the destruction of King Solomon's Temple to 588 BC. Archaeology's date using the Babylonian Chronicle is 586 or 587 BC. Not bad, huh? Concerning creation, Dr. Danny R. Faulkner said Ussher "could be off by a couple of decades either way."[1] That is still closer than the evolutionists' billions of years!

The Gregorian calendar is the calendar we use. It is based on the birth of Jesus. That is why the words Before Christ (BC) or In the Year of Our Lord (Latin: Anno Domini AD) are added after the year. Many experts today think the Gregorian calendar is wrong. They think anywhere from 2-6 years should be added to it.

The same experts point out every calendar has mistakes. What these Christian scholars do agree on is that the history of man dates to slightly over 6,000 years. And this is what the Bible tells us through its genealogies and history.

But the Bible doesn't tell us everything. For example, we do not know how many children Adam and Eve had. We only read the stories of three of their sons. When Cain objected to being driven out of the land where he was living, he said he was afraid someone would kill him. He seemed to be afraid of his other brothers and sisters who were mad at him for killing Abel. Perhaps they threatened him.

Cain moved away and built a city. He named the town after one of his sons, Enoch. Adam's family grew into larger and larger groups. By the time Noah lived, more cities were built. People began spreading out. They farmed, kept flocks, went to markets, made music and fashioned things out of silver, copper, wood, gold and precious stones. But the land Noah lived on did not look like our world.

In 1859, Antonio Snider-Pellegrini realized four of the continents we see today fit together like puzzle pieces. When he read Genesis 1:9-10, he un-

---

[1] Danny R. Faulkner. "Comments on Ussher's Date of Creation." *Answers Research Journal.*

derstood it as God creating one huge section of land. We call this a Super Continent.

Snider-Pellegrini's theory is generally accepted, but his drawing of the land mass is not. Geologists do not think it is what the land looked like in Noah's day. They labeled Snider-Pellegrini's map Pangaea (pan-JEE-yah). They believe Pangaea is what the land was like when it lay under the water during the flood. It had broken and smashed together to create mountains. Pangaea is Greek for entire (pan) Mother Earth (Gaia).

Geologists study the rock layers along the edges of the continents to compare them. What they find are sediment layers on top, the scattered waste of dead plants and animals from the flood, and pure, original rock below. (The original rock is called craton or basement rock.) When similarities are discovered, it helps them determine the edges of the puzzle pieces. The earth's magnetic field and the type of rock found are also clues to help geologists put the continents back together. At least on a map.

Their drawing is called Rodinia (roh-DEEN-ee-yah). It is Russian for "to give birth" and can be used to mean The Motherland. The original rock pieces of the continents form the core of Rodinia. North and South America are two major pieces. But putting all the little pieces together is not easy because there is more than one way to do it. So we cannot look at a map of Rodinia in perfect confidence, but we know Noah's world had land all in one piece in some shape with the oceans around it.

There were grasslands and forests. Some of these forests were tropical-type forests with large palms and ferns. Researchers have found the fossil remains of ancient forests in frozen Antarctica. Professor Erik Gulbranson tells us, "The continent as a whole was much warmer and more humid than it currently is today."[2] Other researchers agree. Studies of fossilized tree resin have shown the

---

[2] Elaina Zachos. "Antarctica Was Once Covered in Forests. We Just Found One That Fossilized," *National Geographic*.

world was warmer, and the same species of insects lived in India, North and South America, Australia and Northern Europe.

But the fossil forests are older than they thought. They are amazed and bewildered at having to rearrange their timeline of events. It may be a surprise to scientists who believe in stages of evolution and millions of years passing before plants grew. It is not confusing to anyone who trusts God's unveiling of the creation story.

Also, what about that fossilized tree resin showing us the earth was warmer than it is today? What does it mean to the modern global warming issue? Evolutionists explain it as an ancient global warming trend 540 million years ago as worms started digging three centimeters into the ocean floor. These creatures released as much carbon dioxide into the air as our burning fossil fuels does today. The event later killed animals. They aren't joking.

In the pre-flood world of Noah there were evergreen trees and bushes, those that had flowers and those that lost their leaves. There were groundcovers and vines, some that flowered and some that had thorns. Plant-eating animals like giraffes, elephants, deer, dinosaurs, rabbits, sheep, rodents and monkeys lived on this land. Meat-eating animals roamed there too like large cats, small cats, bears, other dinosaurs and wolves.

Small birds, large birds, including flying reptiles like the pterodactyl, and bats flew overhead or stood in marshes. The ocean was filled with plant life, whales, sharks, swimming dinosaurs, fish large and small, crabs and other crustaceans and shellfish. There were fungi and bacteria, insects and spiders.

Most of these did not look exactly like modern mammals, birds and insects, however. Fossils from the flood prove this. We must remember that Noah did not take every *species* with him on the ark. He took only male and female *kinds* of every type of land creature, and they created new species. Also the pre-flood world had a mild climate, allowing life to flourish.

Today about seven billion people live on the earth. In Noah's day it is estimated there were around 750 million people. Some guess four billion because of the ancients' long life-spans and the chance to have lots of kids.

What did these people look like? Creationists do not believe man looked like an ape or a chimp. Geneticists say Adam and Eve had medium brown skin with brown eyes and hair. This would supply the genes necessary for all the variations we see today. Remember, none of the people were separated by oceans or vast mountain ranges so genetic traits we see today in a culture would not have been firmly fixed in the people of Noah's day. Genetic research has proved all people carry the same genes to produce skin color. But mutations caused by inbreeding can produce light skin, blue eyes or red hair, for example.

Cheddar Man is named for where his skeleton was found near Cheddar Gorge in southwest England. Recent DNA testing amazed scientists when they discovered he had dark skin, blue eyes and black curly hair. They expected light skin and fair hair. Dark skin types are showing up in unlikely places like Spain and Hungary. Unlikely according to their models of beginnings. They think Cheddar Man traveled from Africa to the Middle East before going to England. But there is no need to place him in Africa first.

One theory from the study of Cheddar Man is that light skin developed because there is less sun in the north. About this scientist Mark Thomas says, "But it doesn't explain eye pigmentation. There are other processes that go on. It could be sexual selection. It could even be something else we don't yet understand."[3]

What they do not understand is the Bible is true. Evolutionists have painted a picture about ancient man that doesn't hold up against the evidence. They <u>were positive t</u>hey found the oldest human remains in Africa because this is

---

[3] Dominique Mosbergen. "Oldest-Known Briton 'Cheddar Man' Wasn't Fair-Skinned After All," *Huffington Post*.

where they believe man began. Close to apes. But scores of discoveries are proving their theories wrong. Even their dates for man. Man, like the fossil forests, is older than they thought. Modern looking men.

Two skulls, one found in Morrocco and one in China, are alike. They are also older than anything found in Africa. In Qesem Cave in Israel a shocking discovery was made. It seems the cave was used as a type of school to teach people how to make flint tools and butcher animals. The real problem is this would mean they had to be smart enough to pass knowledge and be able to speak. They could make decisions, plan, sustain relationships and perform complex tasks and artistry. Archaeologist Ella Assaf says, "… because of such finds we must go further backwards: the more we find, the more we see markers of modern behavior in older sites."[4]

While they continue to try to figure out when man began to speak, we can be assured people looked like people and acted like people because man has always looked and acted like man. And sometimes that can be bad.

Cain's great-great-great-grandson Lamech had two wives. It seems he wanted lots of family. Maybe he wanted to make his name great and have lots of influence. But having two wives wasn't the pattern God gave to Adam for family life. Lamech also talks of killing two men, so we know he wasn't one to honor God.[5] Lamech was not the only murderer, and he was probably not the only man to have two wives. But he was proud of both.

It says in Genesis 5:2 that Adam had a son in his likeness or image. God had said that Adam was created in His likeness. But that changed when Adam changed masters. He was not like God on the inside anymore. Adam's children were born like him. The Bible says Adam passed his sin on to his children when they were born. "…by one man sin entered into the world, and death by sin;

---

[4] Ariel David. "400,000-year-old 'School of Rock' Found in Prehistoric Cave in Israel." Haartz.

[5] This Lamech is not Noah's father.

and so death passed upon all men, for that all have sinned." (Romans 5:12) That is why no one is born good, and why we see Adam's children growing worse in their behavior.

But not all of them. Cain had another brother named Seth. Seth had a son and named him Enosh. It sounds like Enoch doesn't it? Seth and Cain had other children with similar names. When Enosh was born, the Bible says men began calling on the name of the Lord. This means this was the time men began distinguishing themselves from those that did not honor God.

Among those millions or billions of people on earth were some who were strong and very tall. They were called giants and mighty men. Some scientists scoff at this mention of giants in the Bible. It is true no skeleton of a giant has been found. Fossils of giant insects have. That seems worse doesn't it?

A dragonfly with a two and a half foot wingspan, a spider with a twelve inch leg span, a rat weighing seven hundred pounds, a thirteen foot long armadillo and a twenty foot tall sloth are all scientifically accepted giants.[6]

But as God watched people, He became sad. They were becoming increasingly rebellious and violent. Genesis 6:5 states, "And GOD saw that the wickedness of man was great in the earth, and that every imagination of the thoughts of his heart was only evil continually."

We probably do not know someone who is bad all the time. We do not see inside a person like God does. He was looking at what they thought about and wanted. He didn't like what He saw. God was pleased with only one man in the ancient world. This man's name was Noah.

Noah lived when dinosaurs lived. He lived when there were lots of people on earth. He could travel to a town and buy or trade for things like clothes, jewelry, tools and food. He could listen to music or learn something new. But evil was all around him. He chose to call upon God in the middle of it all.

---

[6] Tim Chaffey. "Giants in the Old Testament," *Answers in Depth* Vol. 7.

Noah's World

The story of this sinful world is thought by many to be a myth. But two thousand years ago, a historian named Philo (Fie-loh) of Byblos in Lebanon gathered the writings of a priest. The priest's name was Sanchuniathon (sann-Chew-nee-aw-ton), and he had lived in Beirut, Lebanon, perhaps around the time of Moses. Lebanon was part of the land of Canaan.

Scholars thought the writings were legends. They understood Sanchuniathon to be a mythical person. But an archaeological find at Ugarit (Ras Shamra) offered proof the writings were true and the priest was a real person. Ugarit was an important city long ago in Canaan. Ugarit is in the country we know as Syria.

Sanchuniathon wrote about the early history of the Phoenician religion and the ancient world before the flood. He wrote about farmers, shepherds, reed huts, brick-making and sons who made things from metal. He claimed they knew how to write before the flood. He said their gods were really humans who had died and then were worshipped as gods. We call this ancestor worship. Sanchuniathon described giants. He said people were so amazed at the bulk of these men they named mountains after them.

He said women did not get married but had children with whomever they chose. This created siblings with different fathers. But there was no steady father to lead the family. It created mothers who thought little about properly caring for their children.

He talked about nature worship and said Cain began this worship. People worshipped the sky, the wind, sun and stars. They believed creatures hatched from an egg and some became human. It sounds like the first idea of evolution doesn't it? In fact, he talked about the beginnings of creation growing from putrid water. Some worshipped snakes because they saw them eating themselves. The circle of a snake eating itself reminded them of the cycle of life and death. Parents sacrificed their children to these gods. Murder was common.

Sanchuniathon's writings paint a word picture of what the Bible describes as wicked. The people had become evil in their thinking and daily life. They chose their own way of living instead of the love and honor for each other God had planned.

In Noah's world people lived very long lives. Nine hundred years old was not uncommon, according to the genealogies in the Bible. Imagine your great-great grandfather having kids as old as you. Some younger. Jeanne Calment (zhohn kalmaunt) was a French woman who lived 122 years and 164 days. She was born in 1875 and died in 1997. She is the oldest known person on record. Had she lived in Noah's day, she would have been just a youngster!

Many do not believe people could live to be over 900 years old. But another archaeological find is the Sumerian King List. The first section of the list gives the names of eight kings before the flood and the years they reigned. The scribes who wrote the list recorded thousands of years for a king's lifespan.

The problem with the thousands of years may be that the scribes who wrote the history recorded the numbers using *their* number system which used 60 as a base. We still use a method of it to tell time on a clock. The Bible, however, counts years with a value of one. If the list is read making the changes, the King List and the Bible tell a similar story.

Even if you do not make any changes, the Sumerian King List shows lifespans before the flood were long, and then grew shorter. Also the eight kings in the list represent eight generations. The Bible has ten. If you remove Adam and Noah, you have eight. These eight generations may represent the history after Adam until the flood.

Think about what we have said about the ancient world becoming wicked and what we have learned about the long lives of early man. Do you see how much mischief one wicked ruler could make in the world? Zimri one of Israel's wicked kings reigned only seven days. The army quickly crowned another man which created a civil war. (1 Kings 16:15-20) Ahab was one of their worst kings, and he reigned for twenty-two years. What if such a man ruled 700 years?

It is also true a craftsman would have a long time to practice his skill or try new hobbies and inventions. It makes sense then how civilizations could appear after the flood already knowing how to make pottery wheels, carts, how to farm and craft metal.

Let's sum up what we have learned about Noah's world. The pre-flood world happened around six thousand years ago. There were a lot of intelligent but wicked people. Some of those people were big, giants even. All of the land was in one piece. An ocean surrounded it.

The weather was calm and warm. Plants and animals flourished. It was not a world of complete chaos. There were cities and farms. Businessmen, craftsmen and musicians. People lived in reed huts and possibly brick homes. Men and women were getting married. Some not. They were having babies. Children were learning skills from adults. Adults taught other adults. There were some who worshipped God. There were those that worshipped dead people and nature.

Noah's world before the flood was not a myth. There are geological and archaeological discoveries that tell the same story as Genesis. In the next chapter, we will find out more about Noah and the ship he built.

At left is one idea of what Rodinia may have looked like. Below is one for Pangaea. There may be various stages between Rodinia, Pangaea and the continents we see today. Some call it the Supercontinent Cycle.

• Chapter 3 •

Preacher of Righteousness

When Noah was born, his father was happy that a son had been added to the family. A son could help keep sheep and goats. He could plant and harvest crops. Farming was hard work, and sons were a blessing. Noah, or *Noach* (NO-ăckh) in the Hebrew language, means rest. Noah's father said, "[Noah] shall comfort us concerning our work and toil of our hands, because of the ground which the LORD hath cursed." (Genesis 5:29) Some think Lamech was remembering the promise of a Deliverer made to Eve and saw in Noah this comfort and rest.

Compare what Noah's father said about the ground being cursed to what God had told Adam. Who do you think cursed the ground? Why would Noah's father say God cursed it?

The Hebrew writers use this language to describe the act of allowing. God allowed the ground to be cursed. Many people wonder at this. "Why would a good God allow such a bad thing to happen?" they ask.

To understand this, we need to remember that God gave Adam the freedom to make his own choices, and He gave him dominion. The word for dominion is *radah* (raw-DAW) which means to tread down, rule over, reign or take. God created the earth. He had dominion, but He gave it to Adam. From that point on God allowed Adam to choose how he would rule. But as we've learned, Adam gave it to Satan. God never took back dominion. Instead, He honored Adam's decision. He did provide for Jesus to win it back from Satan, however. That happened when Jesus defeated Satan by His death on the cross.

Eph 1:21-23 says Jesus is seated in heavenly places, "Far above all principality, and power, and might, and dominion, and every name that is named, not only in this world, but also in that which is to come: And hath put all things under his feet, and gave him to be the head over all things to the church, which is his body, the fulness of him that filleth all in all."

Christians are the body, and Satan is under us. *We are sitting in a place of authority with Jesus!* "Even when we were dead in sins, hath quickened us together with Christ, (by grace ye are saved;) And hath raised us up together, and made us sit together in heavenly places in Christ Jesus." (Ephesians 2:5-6) That is why it is said if Satan knew what Jesus' death on the cross meant, he would have never killed Jesus. (1Corinthians 2:8)

Some people say God is sovereign, and He is. But not over the earth. Psalms 115:16 says, "The heaven, even the heavens, are the LORD'S: but the earth hath he given to the children of men." Man has authority if he wants it through Jesus. If he doesn't, Satan is happy to stir up trouble where he can get away with it and blames it on God. Satan has no rights any more. James 4:7 says man can resist him and he has to flee. But many Christians don't understand they have authority over Satan and his works, and they do not use it.

We can know then that God is not a dictator sitting on a throne making every decision. That would make us slaves or robots. We have to read the Bible and know what God's promises to us are. It is hard to rule when you don't know your rights. God is waiting if we ask for His help. He is expecting us to enforce the victory He gave us in Jesus. We have to take our rule. We have to

Preacher of Righteousness

tread on the snake and the lion imitator who roams around seeking whom he may devour. (Psalm 91:13 and 1Peter 5:8) But man's rule is for a time. At some point God is going step in and end this age.

Noah's father did not have any authority over Satan. He lived thousands of years before Jesus, the promised Deliverer. Striving under Satan's rule, he longed for salvation and rest.

Noah did not know how famous he would become. He sat listening to his father and grandfather speak of their amazing family. Noah's family had begun with Seth, one of Adam's sons. Adam, the first man God created, lived to be 930 years old. Noah's great-grandfather, Enoch knew Adam. Noah's grandfather, Methuselah knew him, and Noah's father Lamech knew him too. Lamech was 56 years old when Adam died.

News of Adam's death carried throughout the land. The first man had died; the man who knew God and all about the creation; the man who had stood in the garden and all its beauty. Adam's family mourned his passing. Seth kept the records of his family and their knowledge of God. These records were honored and repeated in Noah's family.

Later another event shocked Methuselah and Lamech. Enoch rose into the sky and disappeared! Lamech was 113 years old when God took his grandfather to live with Him. Nothing like it had ever happened. It was said of Enoch that he walked with God. Before people had called on God, but Enoch loved God deeply, and he thought about Him and prayed to Him throughout the day. God was so pleased with Enoch's faith that Enoch was taken away, and some people saw it.

Jesus and New Testament writers support Old Testament accounts as true when they talk about them. (The Old Testament was their Bible.) Even Enoch is mentioned. But one writer gives us details we haven't heard before. Jude wrote a letter warning about false teachers and those who were against Jesus and

His teachings. He quoted Enoch. "And Enoch also, the seventh from Adam, prophesied of these, saying, Behold, the Lord cometh with ten thousands of his saints, to execute judgment upon all..." (Jude 1:14-15) This is referring to the battle in Revelation 19.

God told Enoch about the end of this age. The Bible says the Lord confides in those who fear Him, so it is not surprising He gave Enoch this information. (Psalm 25:14) Enoch knew of these things thousands of years before it would be written down and given to us.

Enoch was the first person to be described as a man who walked with God. He was also the first person to be raptured. We've already said that he went up to heaven without dying. In the last days this will happen to believers. "For the Lord himself shall descend from heaven with a shout, with the voice of the archangel, and with the trump of God: and the dead in Christ shall rise first: Then we which are alive and remain shall be caught up together with them in the clouds, to meet the Lord in the air: and so shall we ever be with the Lord." (1 Thessalonians 4:16-17)

Noah had never met Adam or Enoch. But he listened and believed their stories and the stories they told about God. As he grew, he saw his brothers, his sisters and his cousins turn from the teachings. They became wicked like their other cousins from Cain's family, and Adam's other sons and daughters.

Hundreds of years passed, and Noah was grieved at the bad things people were doing, things like Sanchuniathon described. Noah decided to be like his great-grandfather Enoch and honor God. Genesis 6:9 says, "Noah was a just man and perfect in his generations, and Noah walked with God."

Webster's Dictionary defines just as acting according to the law or doing what is right and good. Noah did this in the eyes of God. He didn't behave this way only in front of his neighbors. He was just when no one was looking. This shows Noah's devotion to God. He gave God first place in his life.

Perfect in this description does not mean Noah never did anything wrong. Jesus was the only perfect person who never sinned. But Noah did his best to do what pleased God because he feared, respected and honored, God. He believed God would do what He said He would do, and Noah trusted Him.

And he was the only one who did. The verse says he was perfect in his generations. That is hundreds of years. Lots of time to get tired, discouraged and embarrassed of being different. But he remained steady, loyal.

At some point, Noah married. We are never given any information about the woman he chose. Not even her name. But we are all descended from her. Some think she is Tubal Cain's sister, Naamah (nah-am-AW), a woman of importance because she is named in Cain's genealogy. Women were not usually named. Naamah comes from the Hebrew *naem,* and it means pleasant, delightful or beautiful. Noah and Naamah. Sounds cute. But she was born two generations before Noah. Others think Naamah may have been a pagan goddess and therefore not Noah's wife.[1]

Anyway, when Noah was 500 years old, his first son Japheth was born. In all, he had three sons. Japheth was the oldest, then Shem and Ham. It was their turn to sit and listen to their father, grandfather and great-grandfather.

One day God spoke to Noah. God had seen how Noah loved Him and obeyed Him in the middle of the sin around him. God was pleased. He gave Noah an important job. God was pained by the people's violence and evil, and He needed to put a stop to it.

God wanted Noah to build a ship in a specific shape. The ship would need to be strong and not come apart or tip over. When Noah first heard this, he did not know God was going to bring a flood to cover the lowest valley and the highest hill. But Noah listened carefully to God's words and recorded them.

---

[1] Genesis 4:22 *John Gill's Commentary*

"Make thee an ark of gopher wood; rooms shalt thou make in the ark, and shalt pitch it within and without with pitch. And this is the fashion which thou shalt make it of: The length of the ark shall be three hundred cubits, the breadth of it fifty cubits, and the height of it thirty cubits. A window shalt thou make to the ark, and in a cubit shalt thou finish it above; and the door of the ark shalt thou set in the side thereof; with lower, second, and third stories shalt thou make it." (Gen 6:14-16)

The measurements are recorded in cubits. A cubit was used in Noah's day instead of feet or meters. It is defined as the distance from a man's elbow to the tip of his middle finger. You might think that distance could vary with the man. You would be right. Hebrews, Babylonians and Egyptians all had their own standards. Recorded distances vary from the shortest, 17.5 inches, to the longest, 20.6 inches. Egyptians were in the last group.

But none of those people groups or distinctions existed yet. The standard used to build the ark that we can know confidently was Noah's elbow to his fingertip. God apparently knew how long that was because He gave Noah the measurements to use.

Scholars can only make an educated guess to say how big the ark was. King Solomon used a long cubit when he built the Temple. Ezekiel refers to a long cubit in his vision of the Third Temple. That is why the guess is made using a long cubit, a little over nineteen or twenty inches. Other scholars use an eighteen inch measurement.

Using these measurements we can calculate Noah was to build a ship anywhere from 450 to 510 feet long. According to *ArkEncounter.com*, 510 feet is one and a half football fields long. The ship was forty to fifty foot high and had three decks contained inside. It was seventy-five to eighty-six feet wide.

When Noah told his father and grandfather what God had said, they must have marveled at the amazing events happening in their lifetime. The Bible doesn't say anyone had built a ship like that in Noah's day. It is possible that men were building ships. They could have been sailing along the coastline. But the design God gave Noah needed to be especially seaworthy.

The word used to communicate what type of design is *têbâh* (tay-VAH), meaning box. We interpret it as ark, which can also mean a chest or box. The image the word gives us says Noah was supposed to build a cargo ship. Its purpose was to float and stay upright in an extremely heavy sea that had never been experienced before.

People who do not believe the Bible account about Noah state ancient man could never have built a wooden boat so large, and it could have never survived such a flood. They doubt it could float. It is true an American ship 450 feet long and made of wood, yellow pine planks, sank in a storm. It was so long the wood flexed and the ship leaked in a heavy sea. Sailors needed to pump out water when this happened. Unfortunately all the sailors died when the *Wyoming* sank in 1924. It had sailed successfully since 1909, however. The ship weighed four tons empty, but it was not as wide as Noah's ship.

Archaeologists know ancient man was building big ships after Noah. A ship similar to the ark was built by Ptolemy Philopater, a Macedonian king of Egypt. It may have been taller and wider than the ark but about as long. 400 sailors were needed to work the sails and the ship required 4,000 rowers. Philopater was a weak immoral king, and his massive warship was as useless as his rule. But even the crazy Emperor Caligula had a big ship. His was found when Mussolini drained Lake Nemi during WWII.

Pliny the Elder gives us a list of ancient warships in "Chapter 7" of his *Natural History*. One of the ships on his list was described by Archbishop James Ussher in his book, *Annals of the World*. On page 354 he writes:

> "These types of ships were called *Aphracta*, but the largest ship of all had eight tiers of oars and was called *Leontifera* [lee-on-Tee-fairah]. She was admired by all for her large size and exquisite construction. In her were a hundred oars per tier, so that on each side were eight hundred rowers, which made sixteen hundred in all. On the upper deck or hatches were twelve hundred fighting men..."

The *Leontifera* was used in a battle on the Aegean Sea in 280 BC. Ussher tells us this ship performed the best out of all the others. It is estimated to be 400-500 feet long.[2] Many skeptics think Noah would have had to have a ship made of steel to survive his flood. But before *Leontifera*, the Chinese were hardening wood and building multiple deck rectangular ships they called castles.

Archaeologists have discovered more than one ship believed to be the oldest ship ever found. Near Hayling Island in England and in the port of Urla in Turkey, scientists are studying ships they think are 4,000 or 5,000 years old. The earliest ships documented by archaeology were Egyptian. They knew how to use small wooden spikes for nails and mortise and tenon joints. They also used pitch to treat the wood and painted their boats.

We are never told how Noah built the ark. Metals were being used before the flood. Tubalcain was "an instructor of every artificer in brass and iron." (Genesis 4:22) Noah could have used metal in his construction. There is no list of tools, crew or materials. We do know it was made of gopher wood. What we don't know is what kind of wood that was. Jewish tradition says cedar. Others think cypress.

God instructed Noah to coat the ark with pitch. Notice that it says inside and out. The exterior was covered to keep water out. Why the inside was treated is a mystery. To preserve it? To keep it clean? What is your guess?

---

[2] Larry Pierce. "The Large Ships of Antiquity," Answers in Genesis.

When we hear the word pitch we imagine an oil, but it could mean a resin. Pine resin was used in the ancient world to treat boats. One theory as to why the ark was treated on the inside was to make it impact resistant. No stray trees or rocks could assault the floating barge as it rose and fell on a roaring ocean. Modern experiments with wood and concrete coated with a polyurethane showed that coating both sides made the wood and concrete blast proof.[3]

Another aspect is what the word for pitch means. The verse says to pitch it "within and without with pitch." The first pitch, a verb, is the Hebrew word *kaphar* (kah-FAIR). It means to cover but also has the meanings to purge, forgive, reconcile, cleanse and atone. In Noah's case all the meanings seem to apply.

After all the directions, God tells Noah why he needs to build an ark. "And, behold, I, even I, do bring a flood of waters upon the earth, to destroy all flesh, wherein is the breath of life, from under heaven; and every thing that is in the earth shall die. But with thee will I establish my covenant; and thou shalt come into the ark..." (Genesis 6:17-18)

Noah's sons helped him build the strange, huge ship. We do not know if he hired anyone else. If his father or grandfather helped. We also don't know how long Noah took to build the ark. But within a hundred years it was finished. By this we know that Noah was disciplined and faithful to a complicated task.

Imagine the pressure of building something that seemed ridiculous to those around him. *He was building a cargo ship on dry ground.*[4] People probably wondered how he was going to get it in the ocean. He could have surrendered to emotions, but he remained steady, believing God's words to him.

This is what is meant by giving God's word, the Bible, first place in your life. Nothing else and no one else is placed above it. The final authority is

---

[3] Warren Nunn "Noah's Ark—water and impact resistant?" *Creation* 36(3):15

[4] Genesis 7:17 After forty days the ark was lifted up. It would have been adrift before that if it were on the ocean.

what God has said about a matter instead of what the people or circumstances around you are saying. This is walking in faith, walking by the Spirit. It is operating from a place inside you instead of letting your five senses be your authority.

Noah worked hard and was careful to do everything God told him to do. "Thus did Noah; according to all that God commanded him, so did he." (Genesis 6:22) It shows he was diligent and thorough. The Bible repeats Noah did all God commanded him to do. Many times God picked people others thought not qualified. But they were diligent to do what was asked of them.

The Bible says Noah was a preacher of righteousness. (2Peter 2:5) The biblical definition of righteous in the Old Testament is found in the story of Abraham. "For what saith the scripture? Abraham believed God, and it was counted unto him for righteousness." (Romans 4:3)

This verse is talking about an instance in Abraham's life written in Genesis 15. Abraham had a vision in which God told him, "Fear not, Abram: I am thy shield, and thy exceeding great reward." (Genesis 15:1)

God told him that he was going to be the ancestor of so many people it would be like looking at the stars. Abraham made a choice to believe what God said; not what he saw. Abraham was too old to have children. His wife had never been able to have children, and she too was old. It looked impossible. In fact, everyone took it for granted it was impossible. But the Bible says Abraham believed, and this is what made him right with God. It was nothing of his own doing. He just believed God would do what He said.

Noah believed, and he was made right with God because of his faith. This is why Genesis 6:8 says Noah found grace in the eyes of the Lord. The grace was offered to him; he accepted it and believed that God would do what He said. What did God say? That He was going to bring a terrible flood that would destroy everything in the earth, but He would save Noah and his family.

When the Bible says Noah was a preacher it doesn't mean he taught in a church like a pastor. The word used for preacher is *kēryx* (KAY-rooks), herald. A herald is someone who announces official messages of a king or any other leader or military commander.[5]

Noah announced the coming judgment by building the ark on dry ground. Conversations likely followed. In both word and actions Noah warned. Jewish tradition says Noah "repeatedly preached to the children of Cain."[6] It is said he told them if they repented God would not bring the flood. We do not know this for sure. We assume he answered questions asked him. Can you imagine the news buzz his story would have created? Who drops everything else and takes about a hundred years to build a ship on dry ground with no way to move it? Noah, the end-time prophet who claims the end of the world is near!

No one listened to Noah's message. It must have made him sad that his brothers and sisters would not change their ways. Lamech died before the ark was finished. He was the youngest man in the record of Noah's family to die a natural death. He was 777 years old. The number seven means completeness and perfection in the Bible. Perhaps it was a sign that the time was near for God to bring the flood.

Perhaps Noah took care of his grandfather Methuselah. Methuselah was the oldest man alive and the closest to Noah who had known the first man. As Noah saw these things and thought of the destruction to come upon the earth, he must have guarded the family records, and talked often with Methuselah so no fact would be forgotten or story left untold. Then Methuselah died.

His name means man of the dart. *Fausset's Bible Dictionary*, Dr. John Gill and others have said that his name could be interpreted "he dies and it is sent." Considering Methuselah's father was Enoch, a prophet who was raptured, their

---

[5] *Vine's Expository Dictionary*
[6] "The Book of Adam and Eve," *Pirkê de Rabbi Eliezer* XXII

interpretation may be correct. Perhaps Enoch knew of the coming judgment and named his son for it. Methuselah died the same year the flood came.

Noah was 600 years old when his grandfather died. The ark was complete, and God was sending every kind of animal to Noah. This was a confirmation to Noah about what God had told him. His family knew by the animals coming to the ark that the time for the flood was close. How God brought the animals no one knows for sure. Jewish rabbis say angels gathered them or God blew a trumpet from heaven to call them. The amazing thing is they came without Noah having to round them up.

The animals Noah kept on the ark represented families of animals: the dog family, the cat family, the horse family, the deer family, the bird family, the cow family, the frog family and so on. No marine animals needed to be aboard. Creationists estimate there might have been close to 7,000 animals on the ark. But it was not every species of animal as we have learned in an earlier chapter. God was starting over with these animals. They would become the source for the animals that multiplied into all the species of the world today.

God also provided food for them that Noah gathered. One day the animals were all loaded and the food stored on the ark. God told Noah to board the ark with his family. Noah's sons had married, and they followed their mother and father through the ark's only door with their wives. The day had come. It must have been a day of anticipation, fear and wonder. God told Noah in seven days the flood would begin.

The fact the ark had one door is important. It was a symbol to illustrate there is only one way to be saved, and that is in believing what God says and trusting Him only. "Jesus saith unto him, I am the way, the truth, and the life: no man cometh unto the Father, but by me." (John 14:6) Anyone may come to God, but Jesus is the only open path to get there. If any of the eight people disobeyed and never entered the ark, they would have been lost.

There is some debate on whether Noah entered the ark seven days before the rain started or the day the rain started. Dr. Steven Boyd is an expert in Semitic languages. He has analyzed the Hebrew storytelling method in Genesis 7 and says Noah entered the day the rain started.

He thinks the seven days were a process of entering. At God's invitation in 7:1 the process began. Anything that had yet to be loaded, gathered or prepared was done in this time. Perhaps they began sleeping in the ark. We do not know. But we can imagine it was a time of serious meditation. No one probably understood the details of what God had said about breaking open the depths. Noah was 600 years old when the flood started. Japheth was 100.

Were there people watching Noah as he prepared? Were they laughing and teasing Noah about his crazy ideas? The Bible does not say. We assume this because we know human nature. But we don't even know what Noah was thinking.

Perhaps Noah thought of his brothers, sisters, nieces, nephews, cousins, aunts and uncles. He would never see them again. The Bible says God shut the door of the ark. It was a serious event to the eight people inside. They knew what was about to come.

Noah may have been sad for those outside the ark's door, but they, like Adam, had made their choice. Noah hugged his family and gave thanks to God for keeping them safe, for giving them mercy and rest from the trials to come upon the earth.

Seven days. Perhaps it was another symbol of completeness. Perhaps God wanted to give us an example. Jesus, Peter, John and Paul taught that in the last days Christians will be taken to heaven like Enoch. Raptured. Some scholars interpret their words to mean those raptured will be safe in heaven for seven years while evil reigns on earth. After the seven years, Jesus will come, and everyone will be judged according to their deeds.

The story of Noah is the first time the Bible mentions rain. But it wasn't a normal rain like the storms we have today. The Bible says the waters came from above and below. The large piece of land was breaking apart. Water gushed from the openings. The sluice gates in heaven were opened. A sluice is a sliding gate. *'Arubbah* (air-roo-BAH) is translated window. It also has these meanings: lattice, chimney and sluice. A sluice holds back a large reserve of water. We use them today to control water near a dam. The gates were opened and a swarming, frothy tide poured out. It was a rainstorm like no other.

The people outside the ark must have been terrified. They realized too late that Noah had been right. Some of them probably wished they had listened to his message. Nothing survived except the life in the sea, the animals and people on the ark.

1,056 years had passed from the creation of Adam to the birth of Noah. 600 years later in 1656 the worst flood ever to come upon the earth, a worldwide flood, happened. These years are marked AM on the Hebrew calendar like this, AM1656. AM stands for Anno Mundi, and it means Year of the World.

AM 1656 is also the year 2348 BC. People who do not believe the timeline of Genesis, or who do not believe that the story of creation is true, mark the years as millions and billions BCE, Before the Common Era.

Some also believe it was not a world wide flood. But Genesis 7:19 says it was. All the hills under the whole heaven. The earth's layers say it was. (We will discuss that in Chapter 5.)

These people are like those who stood outside the ark's door. They have made a choice not to listen to the words of God. They create their own story. But it is a story they have imagined.

God made a promise to Noah after he left the ark. God said He would never destroy the earth with a world-wide flood again. To seal His promise, He created a rainbow that appeared in the sky. The rainbow is also described as a vision of God's glory, and God's throne has a rainbow around it. (Ezekiel 1:28 and Revelation 4:3) God used His bow of glory to comfort us. It is God's sign to us and should be honored as His special reminder.

In Isaiah 54:9, God made another promise. "For this is as the waters of Noah unto me: for as I have sworn that the waters of Noah should no more go over the earth; so have I sworn that I would not be wroth with thee, nor rebuke thee." God was speaking to Israel. But this verse also points to the promise God made to forgive all the bad things we do if we accept Jesus into our hearts. It is a special time of mercy for anyone who chooses to believe and take Jesus as their Deliverer. We are living in this special time of mercy. Just like Noah when he entered the ark.

But there is a time when this season or age will end. It will be a time when all people have had the chance to decide to believe, to obey God or not. It will be like the day God shut the door on the ark. The Bible talks about this day in Revelation 20, the day Enoch spoke of.

Let us thank God for this special gift of love to us. Let us decide to believe and obey Him now. And when you see a rainbow, remind someone of God's promise to never destroy the earth by a world-wide flood and of His special time of mercy.

In the next chapter, we will learn what happened when the rain stopped.

• Chapter 4 •

After The Flood

Rabbi Eliezer lived at the time of the Second Temple and the early Church. A highly respected teacher, he thought the flood began during the Hebrew month of Cheshvan on the 17th. (Cheshvan falls between our months of October-November.) His friend, Rabbi Joshua disagreed. He thought it began in Iyar (April-May) on the 17th. You may wonder why they argued because the Bible tells us when the flood began. Genesis 7:11 says, "All this began on the seventeenth day of the second month of the year."

Second month, seventeenth day. Simple, right? Except the Jews use two calendars. Civil and sacred. Rabbi Eliezer used the civil calendar and Rabbi Joshua the sacred. Some Christian scholars today side with Eliezer because they think the sacred calendar was not in use in Noah's day. Others side with Joshua because they say that is God's calendar. So, on the seventeenth day of one of those months the flood began in AM1656, 2348 BC.

In the last chapter we left Noah in the ark surrounded by surging waters. But thankfully for us, God did not leave him there. Forty days and nights the rain continued until the earth was covered with water, even the highest points by more than twenty feet. The text makes sure we understand it was a continual downpour for at least forty days and nights. Remember this wasn't a light soaking rain. This was sheets of blinding rain meeting fountains spewing up from below. The land was breaking apart, causing earthquakes, tsunamis and mudslides. As it broke apart, it slammed into other areas creating mountains.

Imagine the desperate attempts as people realized their fate. Were mothers and fathers pounding on the ark's door as they held their children above water? Were the elderly crying for help? There was nothing Noah or anyone else on board the ark could do. God had shut the door.

People and animals on the earth tried to survive. But there was no where safety could be found. They were exposed, depending entirely on their own strength and wits. Genesis 7:23 says, "And every living substance was destroyed which was upon the face of the ground, both man, and cattle, and the creeping things, and the fowl of the heaven; and they were destroyed from the earth: and Noah only remained alive, and they that were with him in the ark."

The Bible says after forty days the ark lifted. The wooden ship tossed in angry waters. For 110 more days rain continued, and the ark floated on a rising ocean. Then the water flows stopped, and a wind came. Genesis 8:2 says, "The fountains also of the deep and the windows of heaven were stopped, and the rain from heaven was restrained."

After the water flows stopped, the ocean level began to go down until the ark hit something and stuck. Noah did not know at first, but he went aground on top of a mountain. On the seventeenth day of the seven month Noah noted. The ark came to a stop in the mountains of Urartu. We say Ararat. Urartu was a region we refer to today as the Armenian Higlands. It includes eastern Turkey, Armenia, Azerbaijan, southern Georgia and northwest Iran.

The land of Urartu or Ararat later became a civilization. It is mentioned in 2Kings 19:36. When the Assyrian King Sennacherib was murdered, his killers escaped to the land of Ararat. Assyria was often in skirmishes with the rulers of Urartu, defeating them only to see them melt into the mountains of their land to rise and fight again. The people are thought to be related to the Hurrians. Ararat was also one of the allied countries to defeat Babylon mentioned in Jeremiah 51:27.

Mt. Ararat is traditionally the mountain identified with Noah and the ark. The location of the ark has been pondered by many explorers including Marco Polo and Sir Walter Raleigh. Other adventurers have made the dangerous climb of Mt. Ararat: Dr. Friedrich Parrot, James Bryce, Aaron J. Smith, Astronaut James Irwin and Bob Cornuke to name a few.

Cornuke has climbed the mountain several times to investigate ark sightings. He and others have found no evidence for the ark. Mt Ararat is *Ağri Daği*, mountain of pain, in Turkey about ten miles from the Iranian border. It is near Nakhchivan (Nock chee vahn)[1] which means place of descent and refers to Noah's family coming down from the mountain. But the Bible does not say the mountain of Ararat. It says mountains of Ararat and seems to indicate a region. In fact, no specific mountain was named Ararat until modern times.

For this reason the search has widened to investigate other sites like Mt. Cudi (KOO-dee) in eastern Turkey. Cornuke has identified Mt. Suleiman in Iran. Mt. Cudi is east of Shinar and out of the Urartu region. Mt. Suleiman is east of Shinar but also out of the traditionally recognized area. Borders of regions were not set as they are today, however. They moved depending on the rulers, wars, treaties, disasters, etc. What is labeled traditional and the expected location of the Ararat region may be limiting researchers.

Jewish tradition says the ark was taken apart by people making charms and idols from its wood. There are scientists and geologists who think the ark would have never survived this long. But, most are willing to investigate any new claims of evidence.

---

[1] The divided part of Azerbaijan on the border of Iran and Armenia.

Noah

God had brought Noah to the place He wanted him to settle and start over. With the ark still wedged in the Armenian Highlands, Noah waited as the wind helped to dry the water. Did you ever notice a wind that comes after a period of soaking rain? This divine wind continued, and a little more than two months later Noah saw the tops of mountains. Forty days later he sent out a raven but it came back because it didn't have anywhere to land. He tried again a week later. Same thing. The next week a dove brought back an olive leaf. Another week and the dove never returned.

About a month passed, and Noah could see land. Almost two months later the earth was dry enough for Noah to leave the ark. But notice Noah waited for God's instructions. He and his family had spent a total of 370 days on the ark. 377 if you include the week before God shut the door.

There are those who debate whether to use a solar or lunar calendar in counting the days spent on the ark. The difference is roughly ten days. If you calculate the times stated, the waters rose for approximately five months and receded for about five months. It took two months of wind to dry the land.

Then, Noah freed the animals. He was careful to release them by their groups as God commanded. Noah didn't throw open the door and shoo them all out. It was an orderly exit. We do not know how long the process took. It seems there were steps taken so the lion-type did not eat the lamb-type as they left the gate. These were the only animals alive to repopulate the earth.

But meat eaters were plant eaters at creation, remember? It was only as the world became wicked, animals started becoming violent. It is possible plants could have served as part of a meat eater's diet. Even today, carnivores can be grouped by the percentages of meat in their diet, ranging from 70% to 30%.

Apparently some trees and plants survived since Noah's dove found an olive leaf. Skeptics think this impossible. But water covered the whole earth for less than a year. There are many ways seeds could have survived, and in his book, *The Origin of Species,* Darwin wrote about his experiments to prove it. What this means is skeptics cannot point to evolution to argue their unbelief because an evolutionist tested the idea and found it possible.

Scavengers had it made. Dead stuff was everywhere. What wasn't floating, beached or stuck between rocks and scraggly tree limbs was buried below layers of dirt. Finding rotting dinosaur carcasses probably kept them for weeks.

Imagine the sights around them as Noah's family stepped off the ark. The earth's landscape was drastically changed. There were new mountains, new plants pushing up through the dirt, swampy areas, young trees and tough ones recovering where they still stood. The weather was still affected by volcanoes and warm oceans. It would be a while before everything settled down and the earth was green again.

The top of Noah's mountain would have been exposed to the elements and harsher than the valleys below. There may have been lingering earth tremors and quakes as the land repositioned itself. Likely, Noah moved down the mountain as soon as he could. At least in the Armenian Highlands he was protected from fierce winds and coastal storms near the ocean.

The area of the Tigris and Euphrates Rivers is called the Cradle of Civilization. It is included in the Fertile Crescent which was in the countries we call Iraq, Syria, parts of Saudi Arabia and Iran. The Cradle eventually spread throughout the Middle East. Traditionally experts believed man first began to settle in this region. But evolutionists doubted that theory and began searching for another.

Evolutionists insist an ape turned into a man near East Africa. They think this early man traveled *from* Africa *to* the land of the two rivers. This is called the Out of Africa Theory. Why this pre-prehistoric man did not develop civilizations in Africa is not explained so well. Africa has several ancient empires. The problem is, they are not old enough for the evolutionists' timeline.

Archaeologists have found towns with the bones of ancient people, their homes, and tools that date to the time this imaginary man-ape is thought to have started his trip. This poses a problem for evolutionists: the African first man was not the first man.

Similar towns and their remains are spread over six sites in Europe and Asia. The discovery of these towns has made the evolutionists' Out of Africa Theory impossible. Some have chosen another site thought to be the place that man began to move over the earth. This site is in the country of Georgia. It is called Dmanisi (mahn-EE -see). At Dmanisi, prehistoric animal bones were found along with human skulls that evolutionists date to 1.8 million years ago. What that means is they are thought to be among the most ancient remains ever found.

For the evolutionists, the problem with these bones is that they are at least as old as any human remains found in Africa. Their own dating methods hint their idea about man beginning in Africa is wrong. What archaeology shows is man, one species of man, in various spots on the globe at the same time. The discovery has brought them much confusion about finding an ape ancestor. They are now searching in China and central Asia for evidence of this man.

Others are not giving up. They think the Dmanisi site are people from Africa. They are convinced they've found proof of evolution. But they have a hard time answering their own questions. Donald Johanson, a paleoanthropologist at Arizona State University wonders, "What was it that allowed them to move out of Africa without fire, without very large brains? How did they survive?"[2]

Indeed. Why would they move out at all just to move back in later?

For those who believe the Bible, the Dmanisi site is interesting. Dmanisi is about 124 miles north of Mt. Ararat. The fact that groups of people with tools and knowledge who lived in various places throughout the Fertile Cres-

---

[2] Ann Gibbons. "Meet the frail, small-brained people who first trekked out of Africa," *Science Magazine*.

cent at the same time points to what the Bible has said all along: Noah's family moved from the mountains of Ararat and spread out from there. Remember, the Cradle and the Crescent are about Noah's family, not the Garden of Eden. Christians know they are not going to find Adam in these villages. People who don't understand the Bible get mixed up on this fact.

Noah and his sons left the ark in the Hebrew month of Cheshvan or Iyar, depending on the calendar used, completing their year on the ark. The first thing Noah did was to worship. He built an altar and made offerings to God. This pleased God, and He told Noah He would never add to Adam's curse already on the ground. "And the LORD smelled a sweet savour; and the LORD said in his heart, I will not again curse the ground any more for man's sake; for the imagination of man's heart is evil from his youth; neither will I again smite any more every thing living, as I have done." (Genesis 8:21)

God also promised that the seasons and days would continue as long as the earth lasts. Some people are afraid we are ruining the earth. But God has promised that the earth will last until Jesus comes again, and then He will create a new heavens and earth. (Genesis 8:22 and Revelation 21:1) We are to take good care of what God has created until that day comes.

God told Noah animals would be afraid of him. This makes one wonder what they were like before the flood. They were tame to begin with, but we know the curse affected people. We assume it affected the animals and assume they became violent as well. Some fossils seem to prove it.[3]

Can you imagine aggressive animals you could not scare away? Some think their new fear was based on the fact Noah had permission to kill them. But that would need to be learned. It was more likely a supernatural fear as a blessing to Noah and his family who were greatly outnumbered by them. It did not mean he could mistreat animals, however.

---

[3] "When did animals become carnivorous?" Creation Ministries International.

God added two new rules to those He had given Adam. The first was permission to eat meat. Of course, it is possible man ate meat before the flood. Jabal is mentioned as having cattle in Genesis 4:20. Perhaps the cattle were used for milk and to make cheese? God only mentioned eating plants in His instructions to Adam. The only allowed killing of animals seemed to be as offerings and for clothing. Self-defense may have been another option.

Also, God knew man would continue to be evil so He gave Noah the first laws. The laws enforced the value of human life and would discourage violence between people. If an animal or a man killed a person, then that animal or person should die also.

When Noah received these instructions, God called them a covenant. God repeated to Noah the other commands He had given Adam. He told them to have many children and to live everywhere on the earth. But one command was missing. God had told Adam to subdue the earth. He told Noah to multiply and replenish it and gave him authority over animals. The ability to subdue the earth was lost until Jesus came and calmed storms. For Noah, the struggle against nature and Satan would continue.

The world outside the ark was harsh compared to the mild climate before the flood. There were no mature forests for wood to make homes or fires. As Noah's family multiplied, they moved farther from the ark. Shelter became rock outcroppings, caves and reed huts. Tools were made from stones and whatever they salvaged from the ark. These men had been craftsmen, and good thing because they needed to be creative problem solvers in their new world.

Evolutionists not only believe early man had to invent language, they believe he had to learn how to use tools. We saw how it surprises them to find what they consider advanced civilizations. But in reality many of these towns they find are people camping out and doing their best to start over in a new landscape. It wasn't that Shem, Ham and Japheth had never heard of metal tools. (Genesis 4) Like the settlers on the American frontier, survival came first. As time went on, these ancient pioneers, Noah's descendants, found ore deposits and improved their living conditions.

Noah lived another 350 years after the flood. During this time he farmed and grew grapes. This is not the first time Noah farmed. The Bible says he was a farmer. (Genesis 9:20) Before the flood everyone had some type of garden and chickens or goats to provide their family meals. But, it is the first time grapes and making wine are mentioned. Taking care of a vineyard is hard work. Grapes grow best where the climate is hot and dry. We know then, he was no longer on the top of the mountains in Armenia. He was tending the earth as God commanded in a valley somewhere. It is interesting that today Armenian wines are famous.

One day Noah became drunk and dishonored himself. He fell asleep naked and uncovered in his tent. The Bible says his son Ham saw this, but we do not know how he knew what Noah had done. Ham told Shem and Japheth who went in Noah's tent and respectfully covered their father. When Noah woke up and found out, he spoke a prophecy over Ham's son.

But it was a curse. Why would Noah curse Ham's son and not Ham? Perhaps Noah saw Ham's son would be influenced by his father? Maybe he said Ham's son would be cursed because he would learn his father's dishonorable ways and grow worse with time. Or there is more to the story. Was Ham's son the first to find Noah? Did he spread the story, laughing at his grandfather?

We cannot know for sure, but what was done was done to mock Noah. The son's name was Canaan, and it was he who was cursed for whatever reason. Ham's other sons, Cush and Put, were not cursed. These boys would be the ancestors of the Ethiopians and Libyans. They would be the families who traveled to Africa. Sometimes this story is called Ham's curse. But now you know Ham was not the one cursed.

Canaan was. Canaan would become the father of the Canaanites. His name means lowland. They lived in the area of modern day Israel, and Syria. The Ebla Tablets and the Mari Letters reveal much about the culture. They were skilled mathematicians, shipbuilders and sailors. They had rich cities but a wicked culture. Shem and Japheth's children would conquer them later in history. The Canaanites' rule would then be limited to what is today Lebanon.

The Bible does not tell us when Japheth and Ham's children were born. It only gives us details about Shem's family because one of Shem's sons was the father of the Israelites. Shem was 98 years old when the flood came. When he was 100, his first son, Arphaxad (AIR-pak-shad), was born. Arphaxad had a grandson named Eber (ay- VAIR). Eber means the region beyond and refers to a land as well as a person. Many of the names in Genesis 10 are used the same way. Except one.

Eber had two sons. About the time Eber's son Peleg (PEH-leg) was born an event happened that changed the world. Eber was so amazed he named his son after it. Peleg means a small channel or river that divides. It can also mean an earthquake or division. See a theme? Genesis 10:25 says, "And unto Eber were born two sons: the name of one was Peleg; for in his days was the earth divided."

Divided? Wasn't the land already broken up and divided into continents and islands during the flood? What does "in his days" mean? To find out, we need to know some history. Using James Ussher's calendar, we know Peleg was born around 2247 BC. The Bible says the earth was divided during the time Peleg lived. Could this have happened again? Yes. But in a different way.

Author Larry Pierce tells us we have historical records dating close to Peleg's birth which give us clues. In 331 BC a Greek conqueror named Alexander the Great visited the city of Babylon. There he met scientists who showed him records dating all the way back to when Babylon began. These records dated the city to 2234 BC. Later Greek historians came up with the same date. This year was thirteen years after Peleg was born. (Remember, the BC calendar subtracts years as it moves forward like a countdown to the birth of Jesus.)

Ancient historians date the beginning of Egypt to 2188 BC. That is 60 years after Peleg was born. Another ancient historian named Eusebius dates one of the first Greek kings to 2089 BC. That is 160 years after Peleg was born. What do the beginnings of these three groups of people, Babylonian, Egyptian and Greek, who speak three different languages, have to do with Peleg and the earth being divided? We are ready to find out.

Peleg was born 100 years after the flood. Genesis 11 reminds us all the people on earth spoke one language. It was the language God and Adam had spoken to each other. God had told Noah and his family to move out into the earth and multiply. But nearly a hundred years had passed since they got off the ark. Perhaps their families followed one of the rivers south out of the mountains. Then they traveled west. When they came to a place called Shinar, they decided to stay. Shinar in the Hebrew is *shene nahar,* two rivers.

Earlier we learned ancient boundaries were not fixed. Today we are used to permanent borders. But ancient borders expanded or contracted, depending on wars and treaties. Genesis 10:10 tells us Shinar is in Babylon. That does not mean the city. It refers to the region of the empire. By that information we know that Shinar is somewhere near the two rivers and in the area of the future empire.

And everyone wanted to stay there. The Bible calls the place the Plains of Shinar. It must have been nice. Fertile ground. Grassland. Near water. A great place to settle down and... never move again. But they were disobeying God's command. They had traveled to this plain from the east. It must have been a beautiful sight to farmers and shepherds, perhaps different from where they had been living in the mountains.

They decided to build a city for themselves. This is the first time Genesis talks about city building after the flood. But this city, like Cain's before the flood, had builders who were disobedient to God.

The people also wanted to make a name for themselves. This means they wanted to be well known. Today when someone becomes famous for something we say they have made a name for themselves. The Hebrew word *shem* (shame) which carries the meanings of a reputation, authority, honor, glory and fame is the word used for "name" in the verse. "And let us make a name[*shem*] for ourselves, lest we be scattered upon the face of the whole earth." (Genesis 11:4) They decided to make a tower out of bricks that would reach into the sky. It could be seen from far away and was their idea of making a name for themselves.

Brick-making was not new. According to Sanchuniathon, people had done it before the flood. But people in Shinar made bricks differently than the Israelites of Moses' day, and Moses, the writer of Genesis, described their method. They burnt them, meaning they put them in a kiln. Israelites and those living in the Promised Land made sun dried bricks and mud for mortar. These people used tar similar to asphalt as mortar. The result was walls stronger than rock.

This type of construction was expensive and took time. It was reserved for important buildings like palaces and temples. Even then the outer walls were built in this manner and cheaper materials used to finish the inside. What the Bible is telling us is this building was important and expensive.

We do not know what they called this tower first. But we know what it came to be named. It is called the Tower of Babel (baw-BEL), and it means the tower of confusion.

You might wonder what the Tower of Babel looked like. Large towers with stairs called ziggurats can be found all over the world. The Tower of Babel probably was a ziggurat or resembled one.

When the people made their decision to build it, they made the decision to turn from God's ways. We do not know if Noah or his sons were among them. We do not know if Noah knew their plans. But God did.

God came down and saw the people's tower and the desire of their hearts. He knew if they continued in their unity, the world would become evil quickly, the same as in the days before the flood. "And the LORD said, Behold, the people is one, and they have all one language; and this they begin to do: and now nothing will be restrained from them, which they have imagined to do." (Genesis 11:6)

In this verse, God reveals how powerful unity is and the ability to imagine an end result. We can practice this to achieve goals and receive answers to our prayers. But their goals were in defiance of God's command.

So, He created a stumbling block for them. "Go to, let us go down, and there confound their language, that they may not understand one another's speech." (Genesis 11:7) The Bible says God confused their language. Groups of people could not understand each other. This was the birth of different languages.

By confusing their languages, God divided the people, and in turn, the earth became divided. This happened during the time Peleg lived. It so stunned Eber, he named his son Division. This is also why different languages such as Greek and Egyptian are dated to the time shortly after Peleg was born.

Did you ever wonder why people from neighboring countries do not speak the same language? Animals do. A buzzard can fly across the border and have no problem communicating with another buzzard. Now you know why.

Evolutionists who study ancient man and ancient languages are confused by the different languages men speak. If man invented language to speak to each other and then moved all over the earth, why don't humans who live in countries next to each other speak the same language? What would be the purpose in not being able to speak to each other? God told everybody the answer to these questions in Genesis 11 and the story of the Tower of Babel.

Today we think of a language like a tree. There is the root from where the trunk has grown to spread out into branches. People who study languages do not agree on the number of roots for language families or language trees. But they know they are fewer than all the thousands of languages that have grown from them. Some think there are twenty different families while others say seventy-eight. All counts seem to be under 100. For example, Indo-European is the root for languages like Irish, Swedish, Greek and hundreds more.

Modern evolutionists are beginning to agree many language roots had their start near the country of Turkey. The land of Shinar, where the people began building their tower, is thought to include the area of northeast Syria. Syria is close to Turkey, and Turkey is where towns began popping up and near where Noah landed in his ark. Unknowingly, evolutionists have uncovered truth.

After God suddenly changed the languages people spoke, they began to separate into groups that spoke the same language and moved away from other groups. Today we know people with similar languages are related to each other. This means God probably kept children and parents together. Also, as people separated into groups certain features got stuck in their genes like skin color and eye shape. One thing is clear: Noah's sons and their wives possessed all the genetic tools for creating all skin colors, hair colors and eye colors. It means these ancient villagers didn't look exactly like each other.

Researchers who study DNA have discovered "the human genome began to rapidly diversify about 5,000 years ago."[4] Genome has to do with the ordering of cells, the genetic information in a person's chromosomes or their DNA sequence. This find has them scratching their heads...again. Why for millions/

---

[4] Jeffrey P. Tomkins. "Human DNA Variation Linked to Biblical Event Timeline." Institute For Creation Research.

billions of years would there be no change and suddenly an explosion of diversity? Putting aside the billions of years, perhaps the diversity came because at first it was just Noah's sons having kids? Then it multiplied, and multiplied, and...

Genesis 10 records what we call the Table of Nations. Many researchers are amazed at how correct this information is about the beginnings of countries and their locations. Some of the countries are still called by the same names.

Skeptics attack the flood story in many ways. One is to say God failed; He did not get rid of evil. He separated the earth twice but didn't succeed. Genesis 6:7 says God wanted to get rid of man. That He did. Except for Noah.

Unity can be a good thing or a bad thing. It is a tool men use to accomplish good and evil. The important thing is to be united with God. Jesus said a house divided against itself fails. If we have asked Jesus into our heart, then we become His house. We are united with Him, and He is united with us. But if we join ourselves with things not pleasing to God, then we are dividing ourselves. Failure is sure to come to us.

God could not bless the people and their tower, no matter how awesome it was, because they were disobedient and their motive was to honor themselves. The different languages were not a punishment. They were God's mercy to a people who had no idea what evil consequences would come from their unified disobedience. Besides Noah, his wife, his sons and their wives, none of these people knew the evil that disobedience had caused in the world before the flood and how quickly it had increased.

In the next lesson, we will learn about ancient flood stories told all over the world.

• Chapter 5 •

Flood Stories

George Smith was born in England in 1840. He did not have the opportunity to get a good education so he went to work at fourteen. But that did not stop him from using his spare moments to pursue his interests and better himself. Skipping his lunches, he used the free time to visit the British Museum and indulge his passion for Assyrian culture. He was introduced to Sir Henry Rawlinson who quickly got him a job at the museum. By 1866 he had made his mark due to his talent of deciphering Assyrian inscriptions. By 1872, he was famous.

He made three trips to Ninevah to conduct excavations. On his third trip, he became ill and died. He was thirty-six. The Queen made sure his wife and six children were provided for.

Among his achievements is the translation of an Assyrian legend found on tablets in the Royal Library of Ashurbanipal. Smith discovered a "mutilated account" of what he said was the Tower of Babel. The inscription was a portion of a larger text he was unable to find. He suspected it had been copied from an earlier source. Smith quoted the story in his book, *The Chaldean Account of Genesis*, in "Chapter X" pages 160-163. The fragment from Column 1 reads:

"...them? the father ...of him, his heart was evil, ... against the father of all the gods was wicked, ... of him, his heart was evil, ... Babylon brought to subjection. [small] and great he confounded their speech. ... Babylon brought to subjection, [small] and great he confounded their speech. their strong place (tower) all the day they founded; to their strong place in the night entirely he made an end. In his anger also word thus he poured out: [to] scatter abroad he set his face he gave this? command, their counsel was confused ... the course he broke ... fixed the sanctuary."

Can you see the Genesis story hidden in the legend? In his book, *The Lord of the Rings*, J. R. R. Tolkien wrote, "History became legend. Legend became myth." That is true of most legends and myths; there is truth buried in them. Back to Smith's Tower of Babel fragment, Column III or V reads:

"In...he blew and ...for a long time in the cities...Nusanner went...He said, like heaven and earth...that path they went... fiercely they approached to the presence...he saw them and the earth...of stopping not...of the gods...the gods looked... violence?...Bitterly they wept at Babi...very much they grieved...at their misfortune and..."

The Assyrian account is not the only story related to the Tower of Babel. In the Sumerian myth, *Enmerkar and the lord of Aratta*, Enmerkar wants to build a temple that comes down from heaven. He says this temple will prosper him and bring him honor. Enmerkar threatens Lord Aratta. He demanded Aratta give him gold for the temple or he would destroy him and his city. At one point a chant is sung inspired by the sorcery of Nudimmud [Enki]:

"may the lands of Cubur and Hamazi, the many-tongued, and Sumer... and Akkad, the land possessing all that is befitting, and the Martu land, resting in security— the whole universe, the well-guarded people—may they all address Enlil together in a single language!"[1]

It seems Enmerkar was hoping to restore unity of language so he could get his temple built. Perhaps you think this myth more befuddled, the truth harder to pick out. But it may provide clues to what happened after the language was divided. Someone still wanted to pursue building the tower for themselves, and they weren't afraid to use force to do it. They had an established religion they created and began calling on these false gods to fix their language. This story may fit with a man named Nimrod. We will talk about him later.

The world tree is another ancient concept similar to the Tree of Knowledge or the Tree of Life in Genesis. In the Hindu version of the world tree, the tree decides to grow into heaven so mankind could stay under its branches and not separate. The pagan god Brahma found out and cut off the tree's branches and scattered them over the earth. He did this to punish the tree for being proud. Each branch grew and became a language. Tower and language legends can be found scattered throughout the earth. For example, Mexico, Nepal, Africa, Australia and Arizona have such legends.

Like the world-wide flood, the creation of different languages changed the world. In our day, computers and the internet are changing it again. The four corners of the earth are less distant. News travels fast. Phone images are instantaneous messages of tsunamis, floods and earthquakes.

As you know, it wasn't always like that. Yes, there will always be people who avoid technology and contact with the world. Some reject it to the extreme like the Sentinelese people on their island in the Bay of Bengal. They are so violent to strangers, they are considered and unreached people group—by their own choice!

[1] J.A. Black, et al. "Enmerkar and the lord of Aratta: translation." The Electronic Text Corpus of Sumerian Literature.

But ancient man did not have a choice. Distance and travel were great stumbling blocks. Even so, Noah's family began with a shared history, and there is evidence of it in various cultures throughout the world.

A world-wide flood would be hard to forget. If you survived it, you would want to tell somebody about it. Noah had plenty of grandchildren and great grandchildren and great-great grandchildren to tell. Add the stories of Noah's wife, his sons and their wives. It would be a grand tale full of details. If you heard these stories, you would remember them.

Did you know flood stories were once told in ancient cultures around the world? Part of Shem's family kept the most detailed record of Noah's flood. Moses used their record to write the story we read in Genesis. Other people told tales that share the main ideas. For example, most ancient cultures tell of a flood that swept the world and covered mountains. They say the flood came because a god was angry with people. The stories speak of a person in a boat who was saved. Sometimes the person in the boat has family and animals with them. Some of the stories talk of giants.

Like the Tower of Babel stories, these details can be found in myths and legends. A myth is thought to be a made up story and uses symbols to teach an idea or moral. Etiological myths are myths trying to explain creation or some other aspect of life not understood. For example, a number of Greek myths try to explain the four seasons. The Greek root for the word etiology means to give a reason for. A legend has some truth to it as we have learned. Also, a legend may feature a hero based on a real person or group.

How do we decide what is a myth and what is a legend? Sometimes by observation. In the Dreamtime Stories told by indigenous people of Australia, modern astronomers understand the stories to be linked to constellations. They labeled one the Orion Story and know that the Emu in the Sky is the Southern Cross. Another example is the myth of the Viking's magic gem which helped them navigate the sea at night. In March 2013 scientists discovered the gem was probably a calcite crystal. Experiments with the stones and a Viking dial proved the sun could be located after dark.

Making your decision about myths and legends can also depend on what you believe to be true. For instance, many experts thought the Hittite people were a mythical enemy of the Israelites. There was no proof in our historical records the Hittites ever lived. Only the Bible spoke of them, and certain experts did not believe the Bible to be true. But when archaeology discovered the Hittite Empire, what was considered myth became legend and then real history. It was Tolkien's process in reverse.

Science, archaeology and history have all proven myths and legends can be based on true events or capabilities. With that in mind, let's take a look at the flood myths.

Africa, Greece, Mesopotamia, Ireland, China, India, Korea, Hawaii, Wales, Norway, Australia, Central America, Finland, and the Philippines are some of the places flood stories can be found. They are also told among South American tribes, Inuit and various Native American tribes. These countries and people groups represent the seven continents of the earth. The stories went everywhere Ham, Shem and Japheth's children traveled.

Many of the stories are still part of native cultures today. South American tribes have a variety of details in their stories. Some talk about an early man who didn't have to farm, angry gods, people who survived on top of mountains and a world that needed to start over because of evil.

The Incas drew pictures that showed water rising above the highest mountains. Everything was destroyed in their flood except a man and a woman who floated on the waters in a box. The wind pushed the box where the Creator wanted them to live. He then fashioned people out of clay and gave them their special languages. Notice they use the word box, the same meaning as ark.

In Central America the Nahua tribe (nah wah; the word means to speak clearly) described the world beginning from one man and one woman. The flood came during the first time of man. Two people escaped in a carved out tree, a man and a woman, and they began the second age of man. The Nahuas are related to the Aztecs.

Other groups of Nahua tribes described terrible storms with thunder and lightening. They said twenty-two feet of water covered the mountains. (The Bible says twenty-two and a half.) The Mayans said the sky fell to the earth.

The Eskimo tell a story about a terrible flood that swept the land quickly and came with an earthquake. People survived in boats on top of mountains. There are many Native American forms of a flood story in the United States and Canada. The Pawnee speak of giants who did not worship the Creator or believe in His ways. The giants did not do what He said, and their behavior grew worse. The Creator became angry. He brought a flood to kill the giants. After the flood, He created more men, but they were small like men are today.

The Ojibway tell of a Great Serpent who kidnapped Nanabozho's cousin. Nanabozho wanted revenge. He wounded the serpent, and a flood came, covering the top of the highest mountain. Nanabozho rescued people and animals by building a raft. They floated for days. They waited for the water to go down. First they saw trees, then mountain tops. Then valleys.

In Hawaii a man named Nu'u and his wife survived the flood on a mountain. Nu'u made sacrifices and the god came down on a rainbow.

Some European stories talked of giants that angered a god. In Ireland, a violent story was told. But two people survived this horrible flood in a boat. The waters drew back, pooling in the deepest valleys which became oceans. Another version of their history says Noah's granddaughter brought people to their land.

Flood Stories

In India a man named Manu was warned by a god of a future flood. Manu survived by building a boat, and it is his children who live on the earth. Among the people on the Andaman Islands east of India in the Bay of Bengal, the flood story said the gods no longer visited the people because they ignored the rules given them at creation. Without warning, the Creator destroyed the earth with a flood. Two men and two women survived. All other living things died.

In a Greek legend about Zeus, it is said he became angry and wanted to destroy all men with a flood. He told his son to build an ark. A few people escaped by fleeing to the mountains. The son and his wife survived by floating on the water in their boat. The son made a sacrifice and Zeus visited him. The son and his wife created people by throwing stones.

There are a few different legends in the Middle East. One is from Babylon. It is called *The Atrahasis Epic* (Ă-trah-hă-sis). This one says the flood was caused by too many people on the earth. One of the gods was annoyed by the noise, and the other gods decided to destroy all the people. One god, Enki, warned a man named Atrahasis who built a boat with plans given him by the god.

In another version, Enki warned a king named Ziusudra. The king built a boat that Enki described to him, and he floated on the floodwaters for seven days. The king opened a window in the boat and offered sacrifices to a sky god. Those who believe the Genesis Flood is a myth think Noah was really Ziusudra.

The most famous Babylonian flood story is *The Epic of Gilgamesh*. The story was carved on stone tablets and sent to the Hurrian and Hittite kings in their languages. *The Epic of Gilgamesh* has a complete set of tablets to tell us the story, but the tablets are worn and some are broken.

In 1853 an Assyrian Christian named Hormuzd Rassam discovered the tablets when he excavated King Ashurbanipal's library at Ninevah. Rassam did not know the importance of his discovery because parts of the tablets weren't translated until nineteen years later. George Smith was the man who translated them. Smith writes that he believed the earliest images of the story were on cylinder seals dating to the kings of Akkad and Ur. Twelve tablets were found, all in pieces. Smith was happy to discover the Deluge (flood) story on the eleventh tablet, the only one in good condition.

The best preserved tablets date to 668-626 BC, the time of King Ashurbanipal. But the story is believed to be much older. Ashurbanipal is known to have sent scribes to other nations to copy their ancient stories, especially Babylonian stories. His library contained thousands of tablets dealing with government, financial and religious documents.

Some scholars think *The Atrahasis Epic* may have been the source for Gilgamesh's flood story. Other experts believe *Gilgamesh's Epic* came first. Both seem to be copies of another source, only no one knows what it is. Christians believe they know the source: Noah's life story told in Genesis.

The main character in the *Epic* is Gilgamesh. Historians believe he was a real king of Uruk. He lived after the flood, perhaps around 2700 BC. The *Epic* begins by describing him as wise and knowledgeable about the countries around him, the secret things, in essence all things. He went on a long journey and brought the people back a story about the days before the flood. He wrote the story on stone tablets.

The journey includes King Gilgamesh searching for a way to live forever. At one point he meets a man named Utnapishtim (OOtnah-pish-tim). This part of the story has many details similar to Noah's flood in the Bible. Utnapishtim plays the role of Noah. He lived in a city named Surripak that Smith said could be translated ark city in the oldest version of the story.[2]

When Gilgamesh asked Utnapishtim, a human, how he was able to live forever, Utnapishtim told him the story of the flood. A god had warned him of

---

[2] George Smith. *The Chaldean Account of Genesis.* "Chapter XI." Page 169.

the coming disaster in a dream. The god told no one else. He told Utnapishtim to build a square boat from a house of reeds, and coat it with pitch. Utnapishtim obeyed. He took all his family, the people who helped him make the boat and his animals aboard. A storm came, and it rained for six days. All humans on earth not in the boat were turned to clay.

On the seventh day the rain stopped. The boat stuck on top of Mt. Nisir in Iraq. After seven more days, Utnapishtim let a dove fly from the boat, but it returned. Next he sent out a swallow, but it too returned. He sent a raven, and when it did not return, he knew the water had dried up.

Utnapishtim offered a sacrifice to the gods. One god was angry that a man and his family had survived. But when another god stepped in to help Utnapishtim, the angry god changed his mind. He made Utnapishtim and his wife like gods and brought them to the rivers. Utnapishtim told Gilgamesh he was not going to live forever. All men die. He told him to go back home. Gilgamesh got depressed, and Utnapishtim's wife felt sorry for him.

Some scholars think the Israelites invented their story of Noah when they became prisoners of Babylonian kings later in history. The scholars believe the Israelites heard Babylonian flood myths while they were living in Babylon and Noah is an imaginary story based on *The Epic of Gilgamesh*. But Nozomi Osanai says there are questions about the flood the *Epic* does not answer.

For example, why did the gods want to destroy all the people? Why was Utnapishtim the only person warned? If he and his wife became gods and went to live far away, who made all the people on earth? Osanai has asked these questions and studied *The Epic of Gilgamesh* in depth. She has written many articles about it and Noah's flood. She points out that 95% of the flood stories told around the world have common elements to the Genesis account but not to *The Epic of Gilgamesh*.[3]

---

[3] Nozomi Osanai. "A Comparison from Secular Historical Records." Answers in Genesis.

Noah

In this lesson we have read a lot of flood stories which show different details of Noah's flood in Genesis. Many of these legends are ancient and cannot be ignored. Some are said to be copied after the people heard the Bible story. Many think they are etiological myths. Of course, not all are believable. Portions of the tales are too impossible to be true.

There is one group of people, however, who were as good at keeping accurate records as the Hebrews. They are the Miao (MEE-ow) people of China. Their method of recording a story repeats itself. The second sentence explains the first by saying it in a different way. This is similar to the Hebrew method.

Their creation story begins, "On the day God created the heavens and earth. On that day He opened the gateway of light." It continues, "On the earth He created a man from the dirt. Of the man thus created, a woman He formed."

About Noah they say: "The Patriarch Lama begat the man Nuah. His wife was the Matriarch Gaw Bo-lu-en. Their sons were Lo Han, Lo Shen and Jah-hu."[4] We can only wonder at Noah's wife's name, but the other names are accurate. We do see that Gaw Boluen is not Naamah. The Miao say the hard rain lasted forty days and another fifty-five as a drizzle.

This is an amazing record, and maybe someday you can read the whole story. The Miao say their ancestor is Gomer, one of Japheth's sons. They list Noah's family and talk about the building of a high tower and how God made languages. The Miao people were telling this story before they met Christian missionaries. By this time you can answer these questions: Where do you think they first heard it? How might they have traveled to China and why?

You may know where the Sinai Peninsula is in the Middle East. It has always been part of Egypt. But did you know the word Sinai can be connected to China?

---

[4] Edgar Truax. "Genesis According to the Miao People," *Acts & Facts 20*, no. 4.

Flood Stories

The Chinese are descended from the original Sinites who lived in the Middle East. Ham or *Han* is their ancestor. The Sinites can be traced to the Shaanxi Province in China which is considered the cradle of Chinese civilization. One of their cities was Thinae, Tsin today, and they were trading partners with the Scythians. Siang-fu is another ancient city. The Bible mentions the Chinese Sinites in Isaiah 49:12. "Behold, these shall come from far: and, lo, these from the north and from the west; and these from the land of Sinim."

Legends are not the only signposts advertising a global flood. The geology of the earth tells a flood story too. Scientists recently discovered crystallized ice about 500 miles below the earth's surface. The study shows pockets of water are also possible that deep. None of the researchers believe it to be connected to the flood story. But the flood helps us understand geology.

If you cut into the earth exposing rock layers in various parts of the earth, thick layers of mud and sand are mixed with fossils and animal skeletons. Rock from the Appalachians can be found in the desert southwest, and sea life is found buried on top of mountains. In the Grand Canyon bent rock layers can be seen, forming the same shape top to bottom as if they were laid down quickly and sagged.

Fossilized tree stumps are found buried. Why didn't they rot? Evolutionists say fossils form under specific conditions. Most form when they are buried before they can decompose. Slowly layers of sediment cover the bones of animals and they turn to stone. But the chances of a fossil forming like this are a million to one. Scavengers, bugs, fungi and bacteria dispose of most dead stuff.

Most people think fossils form over long periods of time. Actually they form quickly if buried and out of reach...like in flood conditions. *National Geographic* reported on a reptile found that was fossilized while giving birth! We know dead animals rot. Scavengers eat stuff. Fossils of perfect plants, ferns and animals don't form today outside of deserts. They can be frozen, but fossils of tropical ferns growing in sub-zero temperatures? In a desert? That doesn't happen today either. Fossils show massive graves that formed quickly. In 2002 thousands of jellyfish fossils were found in a Wisconsin quarry which was weird because Wisconsin doesn't have lots of jellyfish. Not these kind anyway.

Even more weird is a jellyfish becoming a fossil. It is a soft creature which floats when it is dead or turns to goo if it gets beached. Scientists say the fossils were formed within hours from a terrible tropical storm. A tropical storm that sent jellyfish to Wisconsin? Wow. They were found under twelve feet of rock.

Yoho National Park in Canada offers guided hikes to their famous Burgess Shale deposits at Walcott Quarry. They are famous because they feature more soft bodied creatures that became fossils and are thought to come from deep water. Park staff tell you the deposits are changing what scientists think about evolution. Utah also has jellyfish fossil mass graves. So does Australia and Death Valley, California. Do you think it was the same storm?

And then there is Mt. St. Helens. Dr. Steve Austin and Dr. John Morris wrote a book, *Footprints in the Ash,* revealing what they've learned about rapid fossilization, geological deposits, etc., from studying the volcano's eruption. Melting glacier and mudflow devastated the mountain area creating a catastrophe much like Noah's flood. Catastrophists was a word used to describe geologists who believed in Noah's flood. But because of new research, some geologists who believe in evolution created a new name to describe themselves: neocatastrophists. Their catastrophe has nothing to do with Noah, however.

The K-T event is a world-wide mass extinction of 75% of plant and animal life on the earth. Evolutionists say it happened 66 million years ago. The event is recorded in a thin layer of sediment called the K-G boundary. The cause? Evolutionists say a giant comet...and some volcanoes. But K-T is only one of five mass extinctions. Each extinction is named and assigned a time period. In the Great Dying extinction, 96% of earth's species died. Early extinctions involved sea creatures. Later ones involved land animals. The extinctions are separated by thousands and millions of years.

Evolutionists interpret these layers of fossils and mass graves differently. The groups of layers are called the geologic column. Again these layers are separated by millions of years in their eyes. In one theory there are twelve layers. This is supposedly the proof of evolution from smaller creatures to larger. But real science shows mixing of the time periods, one type alongside another farther up on the scale. These are labeled misplaced fossils. The theory is never considered misplaced, however.

In his article, "Five Mass Extinctions or One Cataclysmic Event," Dr. Andrew Snelling says the layers are caused by the flood, and they are where they are to be expected. First the waters of the deep were broken causing surging waters which buried sea life quickly. As the waters rose, fish then land animals and plants were killed. They are found in the upper layers of rock where you imagine they would be.

Creationists remind us none of these layers could have happened slowly. Creatures could have escaped death if they had time to run or swim for it. Instead, mass graves are found. Geology is one science that screams flood, flood, global flood.

Darwin realized the flaw in his theory was magnified by the fossil record. He hoped more research would be the remedy; the missing links would be found, the misplaced fossils explained. But publications like *Darwin's Dilemma, Darwin's Doubt, Undeniable, Heretic, Icons of Evolution* and *Zombie Science* tell us years of study hasn't solved the problem. These author scientists are not all die hard creationists either.

In this chapter we have talked about cultural and scientific proofs for the flood. Noah didn't need proof. He lived it. The only complete and trustworthy account of the flood is written in the Bible. Noah lived 350 years after the flood. Shem lived 500 years after the flood. He died during Abraham's lifetime. Changes in the flood story were already being passed around. Noah and Shem knew the real story. Can you imagine their sadness at the lies? What would they think of our modern theories?

In Genesis 14 Abraham fights a war and wins. On the way home a king meets him to supply his troops with bread and wine. This king was also a priest of the Most High God, meaning the God of the Bible not a made up god. But he was not a priest like Moses' brother Aaron who needed to be from the right family. This priestly king was Melchizedek who lived in Salem, Jerusalem.

Some rabbis believe this was Shem. His name means king of righteousness. Whoever he was, he was important and he worshipped God. There are many lessons to learn from this man. Ours in this study is he was worshipping God before the Israelites were born, at the same time as Abraham and after Noah's flood— in the land of Eber. The true message was being kept by someone and Abraham knew him.

There are people who will not believe a thing no matter how much truth is shown to them. They insist on believing what they have made up. They repeat it until it becomes real to them. In time, others accept the lie as fact.

Ephesians 4:17-18 says, "This I say therefore, and testify in the Lord, that ye henceforth walk not as other Gentiles [unbelievers] walk, in the vanity of their mind, Having the understanding darkened, being alienated from the life of God through the ignorance that is in them, because of the blindness of their heart."

Vanity can mean conceit or excessive pride. The Greek word translated vanity is *mataiotēs* (mah-tie-AH- taze). It means without truth, perverse, weak. This is what our understanding is like when we separate from God and His word. In Noah's day, even after the flood many people turned from truth. The Miao people, who so carefully saved their story of creation and Noah, took the false gods of their neighbors as their own. They did not hear the story of Jesus until missionaries brought the Bible to them.

But we have the Bible. We must make a decision to read it and follow everything God tells us to do like ask Jesus into our heart and to live in love and make forgiveness a habit. If we do we will be wise, like Noah who feared the Lord.

In the next chapter, we will learn about Noah's children and grandchildren and their efforts to build cities.

• Chapter 6 •

City Builders

In Chapter 4, we learned about the Tower of Babel. We said it might have looked like a ziggurat. Examples of ziggurats can be found in Iraq, Syria and Iran. The step pyramids of Egypt and the Mayan temples in Central America are similar to the ziggurats in the Fertile Crescent. The Dūr Untash (dure-OON-tash) ziggurat in Iran is considered the best preserved ziggurat of the ancient world. That may change, however, because Iranians are searching for oil nearby. They use seismic testing which involves shock waves or underground dynamite blasts that could damage the ziggurat. Archaeologists date the structure to 1250 BC and guess it took forty years to build.

The oldest known ziggurat may be in Iran as well. About 400 miles from Dūr Untash, Tepe Sialk in Kāshān (kǎ-SH-ON), Iran is thought to be built in 2200 BC. If the theory holds, Sialk (Salk or SIGH-alk) is older than the Great Ziggurat of Ur which dates to 2100 BC.

The Great Ziggurat of Ur is in the Dhi Qar (THEE kar) Province of Iraq. All ziggurats are big, but this one must have been gigantic. Michael Taylor, an American soldier, got to visit the site in 2008 during the Iraq War. He said the temperature in Ur can reach 120°F, and the forty-five minute walk around the ziggurat is difficult. The first three layers of the foundation are all that is left of the original ziggurat. Most of what we can see of it is a restoration. It was built by Ur-Nammu, a Sumerian King, and his son Shulgi (SHULL-gee). Later, King Nabonidus (nab-on-IGH-dus)[1] discovered its ruins and built a ziggurat over it. Saddam Hussein repaired the staircase and exterior in the 1980s.

Scholars debate how ancient people used ziggurats. But the ziggurats' names inscribed on ancient clay bricks reveal they were used at least partially for religious temples. The ziggurat in Ur was part of a group of buildings used for government offices and a religious center. The idea of religion being separate from the government was not an ancient practice.

It seems ziggurats provided a way for a god to travel from the heavens to earth by means of a stairway or at least by the ziggurat's impressive height which resembled a mountain. Some of the research has shown that ziggurats were built for the god to live in. There were rooms for the priests to serve the god. There were altars and statues. The top of the ziggurat was flat, and this was where the main temple stood. Ziggurats could have two to seven levels. Each level could be devoted to a different god and painted a different color.

In Genesis 28 Jacob dreamt of angels using a staircase to travel between heaven and earth. God spoke to him in the dream, and when Jacob awoke he said, "This is none other but the house of God, and this is the gate of heaven." (Genesis 28:17) He set up a stone pillar and called the spot *Bêyth-Êl*, (baeth-ALE) house of God. This idea of a stairway must have been first revealed before the flood or after. It could have been based on Enoch's rapture.

In the Babylonian story, *Enuma Elish*, a home was made for the gods. "The Anunnaki gods took up the tools, one whole year long they set bricks in molds;

---

[1] Nabonidus was the last king of the NeoBabylonian Empire. He co-reigned with his son Belshazzar whom he left in charge of the throne for ten years. The book of Daniel calls Belshazzar king, but it was thought to be an error until a tablet was found telling the story of Nabonidus' absence from the city. Once again the Bible revealed eyewitness details modern scholars first doubted.

by the second year they raised its head... Inside were lodgings for Marduke and Enil and Ea."[2]

Did you notice it said gods built the temple? In the myth they are called the former fallen whom Marduke freed. They wanted to build a temple for him. Some believe these early descendants of Noah were bringing back gods worshipped before the flood. These gods were fallen angels in Satan's ranks.

Also, remember the eight pre-flood kings listed on the Sumerian King List in Chapter 2? Their names are not the same as the eight men representing the eight generations in the Bible. The King List may be insight into other sons of Adam and their lines. For example, "And Seth lived after he begat Enos eight hundred and seven years, and begat sons and daughters." (Genesis 5:7) Enos is named but the others are not. The knowledge of these other sons, their names recorded in the Sumerian language, may have changed to worship.

As Babylon developed into a religious system worshipping the sun, moon and stars, the number eight is seen repeatedly. The pagan god Shemesh (sun) or Shamash is connected to an eight pointed star. As people migrated after the Tower of Babel event this concept went with them. Chinese mythology refers to the Eight Immortals, and the city of Beit Shemesh mentioned in Joshua 21:16 was a Canaanite city dedicated to the pagan god of the sun. Some people think the Annunaki gods were inspired by the eight kings.

Enuma Elish is a violent, gruesome tale of a female god trying to kill her children. It is called a creation story, but it tells about the beginnings of their gods not the world. A lot of scholars say it is the inspiration for Genesis. How they come to that conclusion requires true ignorance of, or bias against, the biblical account. The title, Genesis, is added to a variety of pagan creation myths such as the Eridu Genesis. None are equal to the book of Genesis.

---

[2] Gérard Gertoux. "Is The Bible Chronologically And Historically Correct?" in *80 Old Testament Characters of World History: Chronological, Historical and Archaeological Evidence.* Page 73.

But back to ziggurats— Moses and Aaron climbed a mountain to talk with God. So did Abraham and Elijah. The Israelites, however, did not build ziggurats. Ziggurat is not a Hebrew word. It is related to the Akkadian word *ziqqurat*, to be high. Moses used the word *migdol* (mig-DOLL) which means tower to describe the building Noah's descendants built. Migdol has the meaning of a pyramid shape and can be used for a strong, fortified place. This may give us another image of what Moses wanted to communicate.

Remember George Smith? His friend, Sir Henry Rawlinson, excavated a ziggurat ruin in Birs, also called Birs Nimrud or Borsippa, Iraq. Today it is called the Tongue Tower. It is thought to be one of the ziggurats that could have been the Tower of Babel. Rawlinson and Smith thought so too, but said the top levels were rebuilt by Nebuchadnezzar.

Etemenanki (EE-tem-en-akee) is another ziggurat in Iraq and another choice for the original Tower of Babel. Its name means house of the foundation of heaven on earth. Nebuchadnezzar II, one of the last kings of the Babylonian Empire, said it was built by an earlier king. He restored Etemenanki because it had fallen into ruin.

The book of Daniel begins during the time Nebuchadnezzar II ruled. One day Nebuchadnezzar had a dream, and he wanted to know what it meant. He called all Babylon's astrologers, magicians and sorcerers to him. But there was one condition. He wasn't going to tell them his dream. They had to reveal the meaning on their own.

Within this drama is one sentence which is interesting to our study. It shows what they knew about their gods. Daniel 2:11 says, "... it is a rare thing that the king requireth, and there is none other that can shew it before the king, except the gods, whose dwelling is not with flesh." The astrologers, magicians and sorcerers claimed their gods did not live among them. But it seems the people wanted them to because they built rooms for them in the ziggurats.

The God of the Bible walked with Adam. His presence was known by Enoch. He spoke to Cain. He spoke to Noah. He would travel with the Israelites in the desert. He would dwell in the Tabernacle and the Temple. He would be called Emmanuel, God With Us. John would write, "... the Word was God...And the Word was made flesh, and dwelt among us." (John 1:1 and 14.) With this in mind, a ziggurat is an image of an ancient, unbelieving man's desperation and longing for a god who loved him and would help him.

Although a video on the Smithsonian Channel claims the Tower of Babel has been found, it hasn't. The Tower of Babel Stele featured in the video shows Nebuchadnezzar's rebuilt temple. His cannot be the Genesis tower because it was built one hundred years after the flood, (2250 BC) and hundreds of years before Nebuchadnezzar was born!

But in the video, Dr. Andrew George from the University of London says Nebuchadnezzar's ziggurat inspired the Bible's Tower of Babel story. That's impossible. He says that because the Jews were captives in Babylon under Nebuchadnezzar II. But in 605 BC! Nebuchadnezzar I reigned during the Middle Babylonian period. He built a temple in Nippur for the god Enlil around 1124-1104 BC. Neither Nebuchadnezzar could have built the original tower.

Just so we know the facts, the Bible never calls the tower, the Tower of Babel. It says, "And they said, Go to, let us build us a city and a tower... And the LORD came down to see the city and the tower." (Genesis 11:4-5) It also doesn't tell how big it was. All we know for sure is it was taller than the buildings around it. The Bible doesn't name the Tigris and Euphrates Rivers. It tells us the people "builded" the tower and were working on the city. The city was not finished at the time God confused the languages.

There are a total of nineteen towers or ziggurats in Mesopotamia. Another ten are described in ancient texts. They are found from the north in Mari, Syria to Khorsabad, Iraq to Eridu (air-REE-doo) near the Persian Gulf and over to

Susa in Iran. The city of Kish (also called Cush) in Iraq had three. We've already learned about the most famous ones of archaeology.

What archaeologists are struggling to understand is where were they first? Some scholars date the invention of the ziggurat to the time of the Ubaid (oo-BADE) people. The Ubaid are not a mysterious people who suddenly appeared in Mesopotamia. They are the children of Noah's children and their children and their children... You get the idea. They were multiplying in number; the population of the world after the flood was growing. They were spreading out a little to allow room for their flocks and herds. But they stuck to the river valleys and not too far from each other. Let's take a look at the migration of Noah's family as they moved about the region.

A culture supposedly dating to 6,000 BC is the Halaf (HAL-uf) people. They seem to have migrated south out of the Armenian Highlands into Turkey, Syria and Iraq. They raised cattle, sheep, goats and knew how to adapt farming methods to the dry climate. They grew wheat, barley and flax.

Another group that came after them was the Ubaid culture. Both cultures built round or rectangular mud-brick homes with multiple rooms. Their homes were constructed on stone foundations, and their villages were unwalled, suggesting peaceful relations with others. There were craftsmen who worked with metal. There were weavers and pottery makers who made various forms of pottery. They painted and decorated with geometric designs or drawings of animals. The craftsmen made these products for home use and trade.

The Halaf and Ubaid cultures are thought to be older than the people who developed the cities of Shinar into an empire. This makes sense if you realize they were moving out of the mountains of Ararat. It doesn't if you believe something else.

While civilization actually began before the flood in Eden and east of it, the traditional view is civilization started in southern Iraq and spread north.

This opinion is influenced by Genesis 10:10 describing Nimrod's territory. All the cities are identified as being in the area of Baghdad. It is true this is where archaeology finds the ancient cities located. But this is where large scale city development began after the flood.

The above two statements are important. Civilization had already been Noah's experience. It was his family's experience. It existed before the flood, and shows up where the people and Ham, Shem and Japheth eventually wanted to build it. It appears because of location and desire.

The Bible says the people came to Shinar from the west, and we know then they traveled south out of the Armenian Highlands. And, not surprisingly to those who believe the Bible accurate, recent discoveries indicate civilization began near the Caucasus (KAW-keh-sis) Mountains and spread south. This would explain the Halaf and Ubaid people and their villages.

Researcher Anne Habermehl states that Shinar, the land of the two rivers, included the northern plain near Tell Brak Syria as well as part of Iraq. She also thinks Babel may not have been the city that came to be called Babylon. *Bâlal* (bah-LAL) is the Hebrew word used for confused. Babylon did have ziggurats, but she thinks it may not have been where the Tower of Babel was located. Other respected archaeologists are considering her research.

Either way you look at it, the Bible connects confusion with Babylon. *Easton's Bible Dictionary* defines Babylon as the Greek form of the Hebrew *bâbel* (bah-VEL). *Easton's* quotes the Assyrian definition of Babylon as, "The city of the dispersion of the tribes."

Note that it says city. The Bible says the people made a building and a city. The Akkadian language is the source used to translate Babylon as Gate of the Gods. According to *Strong's Concordance,* Babel comes from *bâlal* and is used 260 times in the Bible for Babylon. It is used only twice for the tower and the city in Genesis 10 and 11. "Therefore is the name of it called Babel; because

Noah

the LORD did there confound [*bâlal*] the language of all the earth." (Genesis 11:9) Thus Babylon and Babel are both confusion.

We know from the Bible Shinar was an array of settlements which became Babylon, the empire. Kingdom building, however, came after the Tower of Babel event. "And the beginning of his [Nimrod] kingdom was Babel, and Erech, and Accad, and Calneh, in the land of Shinar." (Genesis 10:10) Akkad is thought to have been to the north of Babylon. Its name is mentioned over a hundred times in cuneiform, but it has never been found. In fact, only one city on the list is known for sure: Erech or Uruk.

To sum up, 1.) No one *really* knows where the city of Babel is, 2.) We know the Bible links Babel and Babylon together in the land of Shinar, 3.) There may be an original city of Babel we have yet to uncover because Shinar included the northern plains, 4.) Points 1 and 3 may be wrong.

Confused? That's our Tower!

We do have some clues. Uruk was a city in Sumer. When archaeologists and anthropologists speak of Sumer, they are referring to the whole region because Sumer was an early empire we can locate beyond doubt... mostly. There are two stories of how the people came into Sumer, especially into the ancient cities of southern Iraq. Both could be correct.

One story is of a people who call themselves the black headed people. They say they came from the north, an area we identify today with the Caucasus Mountain Range which includes the Armenian Highlands. Another is they came from the east and joined Semites who were already settling in the plains. Putting the stories together shows the movement of Noah's sons' families who came south and possibly united when they traveled west.

Then there is the Sumerian Problem. Dr. Charles Aling states the Sumerian language was not related to another language from which it borrowed words. But it does not appear any new people arrived in the Ubaid or Halaf settlements speaking Sumerian. There is no proof of different pottery styles, and their myths are the same as the rest of the region. Archaeologists conclude from this there is no Sumerian race. But people living there became Sumerian.

Hm-m. That is significant. But— secular experts do not connect the information with the Genesis 11 language explanation.

So where is the tower? The Tower of Babel according to the Bible is connected with a city. We assume the city is Babylon. The Bible says the people didn't finish the city, but we assume Nimrod took up where they left off because one of his cities is named Babel.

Eridu is today's Abu Shahrein, Iraq, about fourteen miles south of Nasiriyah and thirteen miles south of Ur. Sumerian scribes said it was the oldest city in the world. It is thought to date to 5400 BC. Eridu was the source of the first pagan flood story, the *Atrahasis Epic*. It has a story describing a garden much like the one in Eden. The earliest evidence of sailing boats is found in Eridu and dates to the Ubaid people.

It also has a ziggurat dating to the Ubaid culture and, this is important, before the Sumerian culture. Cuneiform tablets call it Nun-Ki or Mighty Place. Nun-ki is also used for the word Babylon. Berossus, an ancient Babylonian historian, calls Eridu Babylon. The Sumerian King List states it was where "the kingship descended from heaven."[3]

Two ancient myths seem to indicate Eridu. Its tower and city were abandoned. In one myth the goddess Inanna stole the sacred decrees from Eridu and took them to Uruk.[4] Eridu covered about 100 acres and thousands of people lived there. Is Eridu Babel? Eridu is a good candidate. We assume one of the towers in Babylon is built over the original. Or, perhaps we have never found the original like Anne Habermehl suggests.

---

[3] Joshua J. Mark. "Eridu." Ancient History Encyclopedia.

[4] Joshua J. Mark. "Inanna," Ancient History Encyclopedia.

One thing we don't have to puzzle over: the idea of ziggurats caught on and was taken with people as they traveled from Babel. That is why you find them scattered over the earth.

When archaeologists find settlements and cities everywhere at the same time, they are witnessing what is called the dispersal, the scattering of the people after their languages were divided. They label it the Uruk Expansion and assign it a period, the Uruk Period. They place it after the Ubaid Period. In the Uruk Expansion space of time, they list the rise of civilization and the skill of writing. But their reasons for the expansion differ from the Bible. They say trade and the need for goods created the expansion.

The Bible insists people did not want to separate. Expansion, trade and widespread wealth and civilizations followed their forced separation at Babel. Some settlements included in this period are Hacinebi and Samsat in Turkey, Jebel Aruda, Tell Brak and Habuba Kabira in Syria, Gesher Benot Ya'aqov in Israel (creationists' view), Godin Tepe, Chogha Mish and Susa in Iran.

Finds in Çatalhöyük (chatl-HOYUKE) Turkey and Ain Ghazal (INE ckha-ZEL) Jordan have shown that farming was part of the ancient world when evolutionists expected people to only know how to hunt and gather food. Evidence of sheep, goats, two kinds of wheat, almonds, peas, lentils and vetch have been found at the site.

Facts show man was farming all over Mesopotamia and beyond. Along the Sea of Galilee in the Jordan Valley the Ohalo II village was discovered. They date this village to 23,000 years ago. Ohalo II reveals people were fishing and harvesting grains, vegetables and fruits. Professor Sternberg stated, "Those early ancestors were more clever and more skilled than we knew."[5] These types of settlements can be found in Europe, Africa, China, Central and South Asia, in Peru at the Caral-Supe site and even in Michigan and Wisconsin. But the

[5] "Scientists Find Evidence of Small-Scale Farming 23,000 Years Ago in Israel." Science News.

City Builders

agricultural revolution as it is called began in Mesopotamia, and according to genetic research of plants burst on the scene in Turkey, Syria, Iran and Iraq at the same time. Some ancient crops are still eaten today. Others like knotweed and goosefoot found in America are considered weeds.

Trade was important. Egyptians needed resin to embalm their dead. Kings, jewelry makers and artists needed gold and gemstones. People living in Turkey were trading obsidian, a volcanic rock for making knife blades, to farmers in Jericho a thousand miles away. Migration caused a desire for things people missed from their old home regions. It caused new resources to be discovered and traded for increased profit.

The so called Uruk Expansion confuses experts who believe in evolution or do not believe the Bible is accurate. They are trying to find out how people learned to farm and how the skill passed to other people. So far, they have no answers, just farmers dating back 10,000 years plus by their calculation.

Another interesting find which shows an advanced ancient man involves a murder mystery. The frozen victim was called Ötzi, named for the Ötzal Alps where he was found on Similaun Mountain near the border between Italy and Austria. He was outfitted well for the harsh terrain. He used bear skin, deer skin, cow leather, fur, grass and tree bark to make his clothes and waterproof shoes. He carried medicinal plants and ate meat and bread. Like any good outdoorsman, he also carried an axe, a knife, a kit for making fires, a bow with arrows and spare string.[6]

A closer look hinted at something not quite right. He had cuts on his chest, wrists and hands. He had bruises on his body, and a head injury. He seemed to have been in a fight for his life. An arrow embedded in his shoulder said he lost. He was shot in the back and bled to death quickly. The reason for his violent death is not clear.

---

[6] "A Glimpse into Life after Babel," *Answers Magazine* Volume 12.3 pg 40.

Theft was not a motive because his axe, a finely crafted copper one from what is today central Italy, was valuable. Modern researchers think he may have been murdered by someone he knew. He had recently eaten a good meal, not running from anyone apparently, and the shaft from the arrow was missing. Of course, the murderer may have just wanted to reuse the shaft. Who killed him and why we will probably never know.

But Ötzi shows us many things about people living close to the time of Babel. Evolutionists consider the time between Babel and Abraham a mysterious unknown. Here we see Ötzi was well able to think, plan and provide. He may have been employed as a trader or shepherd. Ötzi had many skills common to modern man and even his problems.

Some people cannot imagine Noah's family multiplying so quickly in hundreds of years. But Genesis 11 shows us men began having children in their thirties and died when they were two hundred years old. That is a long time to have lots of children. At Çatalhöyük two thousand homes were discovered. Archaeologists have dated these early discoveries 10,000 years or 23,000 years ago. But man has only lived for a little over 6,000 years. The flood happened in 2348 BC, the Tower of Babel around 2250 BC.

The Bible does not agree with their time line. But their discoveries do not contradict what the Bible says. Instead it provides a framework. The Bible states Noah's family migrated out of the mountains in the region of Ararat, an area between the Black and Caspian Seas which stretched south. It next places them in the Plains of Shinar.

The land was harsh at first, the living simple, and in time they improved their circumstances. While not all the locations of the towns have been found beyond doubt, Erech (Genesis 10:10) is Uruk or Tall al-Warkā. The earliest parts of the city date to the time of the Ubaid people. Uruk is north of Eridu. It also dates to the time of the Ubaid.

These cities tell us an important detail: Noah's family traveled south. They traveled together, some ahead (Halaf), some behind (Ubaid) until they came together and stopped in this fertile region. The earliest settlements are found on this route. The decision was made to create a gathering place and to make a name for themselves.

If archaeologists interpret the earliest cities of the Ubaid and the following Uruk Expansion correctly, they were religious shrines and a place to have feasts. Villages were built nearby, separate from the holy site. DNA testing has shown people in Ireland, Greece, Europe and India share ancestors with these early farmers. This is not amazing if you read Genesis. It already said that.

In Genesis 10 a list of Noah's sons and grandsons is given. Genesis 10 actually happened after Genesis 11. We know this because Genesis 10:5 says, "By these were the isles of the Gentiles divided in their lands; every one after his tongue, after their families, in their nations." Different languages or tongues did not appear until Genesis 11. Again, this is the Hebrew storytelling method. First comes general information and then the details why language changed.

The list in Genesis 10 is important because it tells us the beginnings of nations and countries. Adam's sons have Hebrew names. Hebrew names are used until we come to the list of Noah's great-grandsons. Gomer is one of Japheth's sons. In Genesis 10:3, Gomer's sons are the first to have names that are not Semitic. This is a clue to the timing of the Tower of Babel.

Japheth's descendants settled regions of the north, near the Black and Caspian Seas and beyond. They migrated to present day Germany, France, Wales, Ireland, Russia, Georgia, Turkey, Greece, Cyprus, India, Ukraine, Romania, China, England, Iran (Medes and the Persians), Spain and Armenia. They are also ancestors of the Thracians from the former Yugoslavia.

Ham's children and grandchildren settled in present day Egypt, Libya, Ethiopia, Sudan, Iraq, the Persian Gulf area, Greece including Crete (also

Philistines), Arabian Peninsula, Sinai Peninsula, Japan, and the mixed tribes of Canaan which included territory in Lebanon, Syria, Jordan and Israel and mixed people like the Hittites, Amorites, etc.

Shem's descendants settled in present day Syria, Iraq, Iran (Elamites), Western Turkey (Lud/Lydians) and Arabia. Later they took over Canaan.

Japheth's descendants are made up of the Aryan and Indo-Europeans. Shem's family is called Semitic. Ham's is African and Semitic because Shem and Ham shared regions. As you can see territories overlapped, people mingled and married. Today DNA tests are showing traces from each son in many people. Even so there is much written about mitochondrial DNA, genetic diversity and origins of different species of man. Supposedly the research proves there was more than one evolution, and all of us are African.

If you read an article, you might think the results are stone cold fact. But check the details and you find the information is based on chain after chain of assumptions rooted in evolution, none of it ever proven. There is no outside proof of their claims either. You also find honest evolutionists who will not validate the claims until there is concrete evidence. Creationists point out what they are studying is migrations not origins. Other studies, as we have learned, agree.

Migration created settlements and eventually countries. All modern countries are descended from the seventy nations in Genesis 10, the Table of Nations. Many scholars have been amazed how accurate this information has proved. It would be difficult, perhaps impossible, to piece this information together on our own. It is not a list confused with mythical beings or legends like Sumerian or Greek history. It is list of real people who settled real places. Professor William F. Albright, respected archaeologist and biblical scholar, said, "The Table of Nations remains an astonishingly accurate document."[7]

---

[7] William F. Albright, *Recent Discoveries in Bible Lands*. Page 25.

City Builders

The names listed can be a region, a tribe and a migration. Some of the sons and grandsons are identified with towns, islands or legends. Josephus identified Uz, a grandson of Shem, with founding Damascus. Japheth's son Magog is connected to the Goths. His other son Meshech built Moscow. Non-biblical sources say Japheth's son Tiras was worshipped as Thor the god of thunder. Javan is the father of Greeks, and his son Dodan fathered the legendary people of Troy. Asshur is the ancestor of the Assyrians and the name of their chief god.

The list in Genesis was written by Moses when he was leading the Israelites in the desert. But people continued to move and settle and conquer lands. Some countries and kingdoms have come and gone like they do in modern times. Think how the countries have changed in Africa or the old Soviet Union. Countries in the Middle East were created after WWI. Even today ambitious rulers, wars and natural disasters can change the political landscape.

Speaking of an ambitious ruler, perhaps the best known city builder and legend among Noah's family is Ham's grandson Nimrod. "And Cush begat Nimrod: he began to be a mighty one in the earth. He was a mighty hunter before the LORD: wherefore it is said, Even as Nimrod the mighty hunter before the LORD. And the beginning of his kingdom was Babel, and Erech, and Accad, and Calneh, in the land of Shinar." (Gen 10:8-10) And so begins the history after the Tower of Babel according to Genesis.

In the next chapter, we will take a look at Nimrod and someone who seems to be a lot like him.

• Chapter 7 •

Empire Builders

The Sumerian King List was found in Nippur, Iraq in 1906. The most complete version of the List is a stone cube eight inches tall with cuneiform writing on its sides. It is chipped, cracked and worn in spots. It is thought that the hole running through the center of the cube was for a spindle so the cube could be turned and read easily. The List is a type of recorded history, like our Presidents' names and years in office written in a book. Historians believe the List to be a mix of myth and real kings with real reigns.

Most of the myth thinking falls into the section of history before the flood. We have already learned the eight pre-flood kings had reigns lasting thousands of years according to our reading of their number system. Are there any other hunches about these years? Yes. Historians have a unique explanation for the thousands of years. They say the long reigns were a way to describe how powerful a king was. But, they have no explanation why that descriptive writing method changed for the kings after the flood.

Evolutionists face big challenges with the King List. They date the List to around 266,000 years ago. But they think apes became men around 200,000 years ago. Here then is a list of men before men were formed. Well that doesn't work does it? Even worse, they date the rise of civilization, including king types, to around 6,000 years ago. This creates another problem.

To solve it, they say there was a pre-Adamite civilization which became extinct. When they say Adam they mean the ape-man and say archaic human. Another angle leading to this conclusion is connected to DNA research. Tests were expected to show all DNA going back to one ancestor in Africa, the ape-man Adam of the evolution scenario. What the testing did prove was a link to another ancestor much older.[1]

It seems like a slam dunk for the biblical Adam or Noah. But creationists do not believe evolutionists could or would interpret human fossils from the flood correctly, if such evidence could be found. Their bias against the Bible would prevent it. They dismiss the biblical Noah and reinvent Adam.

In conclusions concerning the DNA tests we see this opinion played out. A link to ancestors evolutionists understand as extinct are explained as modern humans on the List marrying ape humans 195,000 years ago. But we are left wondering about the "modern" humans on the List, where they came from and why did they become extinct? Evolution complicates man's history. Anyway, the Sumerian King List has been studied for a hundred years, and evolutionists have found no true answers on that subject either.

There are other interesting things mentioned in the List, however. In the pre-flood history, the city of Eridug is said to be the place kingship began. Eridug is Eridu. After this listing of eight kings it says, "Then the flood swept over."[2] The List also recorded kings in the cities after the flood. The first city was Kish or Cush. This was not the region in Africa. That settlement would come later as people migrated there. The List says, "After the flood had swept over, and the kingship had descended from heaven, the kingship was in Kish."

---

[1] Alan Boyle. "African-American's Y chromosome sparks shift in evolutionary timetable."
[2] "Sumerian King List," Wikipedia

Kish, Uruk, Ur and Akkad are among the regions on the List.

Henry Rawlinson concluded from his research the Semitic and non-Semitic speakers who founded Mesopotamia were both black skinned and called themselves black heads. (Remember Cheddar Man?) He considered them Cushites. Some modern scholars agree. They see the early written language or statues of kings and others with painted skin or curly hair as proof. King Gudea of Lagash is an example. We may conclude then that the Cushites began the Sumerian civilization, and later some of them traveled to Ethiopia.

We observe from the List a city-state system. There are settlements and there are kings ruling them alongside each other's territory at the same time. This makes it hard to establish a chronology. It also shows the settlements fought wars with each other. Sometimes the rulers lost the kingship in their city, and it was "moved" meaning the conquering king governed from his city.

Many of the kings listed after the flood were thought to be made up too, part of a collection of mythical tales. There is a number of interesting Cushite kings. Etana is called the shepherd who rose to heaven and united the surrounding cities. A legend tells us he desperately wanted children and helped an eagle who was attacked by a snake hiding in the belly of a bull. The eagle gave him a birth plant. Illustrations of this story have been uncovered in Iran, and the story was found in Susa, Assur and Ninevah.

Enmebaragesi (En-mee-bar-GEE-zee) is the earliest Cushite king to be confirmed as a real ruler. He is mentioned in the Tummal Chronicle and elsewhere as being a king. The Sumerian King List says he was defeated by Dumuzid the king of Uruk. Gilgamesh, who reigned after Dumuzid, called Enmebaragesi a woman in his *Epic*. Apparently that was an insult.

Speaking of Gilgamesh, two of the myths we learned about are connected with the Sumerian King List. One is a tower myth and the other is a flood myth. Both myths involve kings of Uruk.

Noah

In a previous chapter we learned Enmerkar (*Enmerkar and the Lord of Aratta*) wanted to build a temple for the god Enki at Eridu. His Eridu must have been named after the pre-flood city of Eridug. Someone wanted to tap Eridug's honored reputation and bestow it upon the new one. According to all myths about Enki, the new Eridu was his home. We talked about Enmerkar's prayer for man to speak one language again. The god Enki had changed one language into many because of ambitious lords, princes and kings.

Most thought this story was complete myth. But Enmerkar is among the kings on the Sumerian King List. He is named as the second king of Uruk and its builder. His father, the first king, "entered the sea and disappeared."[3] Enmerkar's story included the Lord of Aratta. Another discovery, *Enmerkar and En-suhgir-ana*, revealed this ruler's name: Ensuhkeshdanna. Now you know why we call him Lord Aratta. There are a few myths describing Enmerkar's battles with Lord Aratta.

Lugalbanda Epic is another story featuring Enmerkar and his soldier Lugalbanda. In *Lugalbanda in the Mountain Cave,* Lugalbanda becomes ill during the fight with Aratta but recovers. He helps Enmerkar defeat Aratta in *Lugalbanda and the Anzud Bird*. He is called the Shepherd and is listed as a king after Enmerkar on the List. Historians understand these events as real battles with real people from real places.

But archaeologists ask where is Aratta? According to the stories it was a rich place full of artisans, gold, gems and lots of lapis lazuli. In 2000 a flash flood in Iran revealed a huge archaeological find in the Jiroft region of south central Iran. Yousef Madjidzadeh, an Iranian archaeologist, thinks it may be Aratta. Dr. Yuri Shilov thinks it is in the Ukraine. He wrote a book about it, *Ancient History of Aratta-Ukraine (20,000 BCE - 1,000 CE)*. Another possibility? The name could be a version of Ararat. Aratta is most likely a real place,

---

[3] "Sumerian King List," Wikipedia

and Enmerkar and Ensuhkeshdanna real rulers. Giving the theory weight is kings listed later on the tablet are confirmed rulers.

We also learned about Gilgamesh and his flood story in the *Epic of Gilgamesh*. He was the king of Uruk or Erech as the Bible spells it. (Iraq comes from the word Erech.) And guess what? Gilgamesh is listed as the fifth king of Uruk on the Sumerian King List. It also calls him the Lord of Kulaba. So does the story *Gilgamesh and Aga*. "Gilgamec, the lord of Kulaba, placing his trust in Inana, did not take seriously the advice of his city's elders."[4] Aga was the king of Kish, also named on the List.

The *Epic of Gilgamesh* is said to be the original story of the flood, and the Hebrews copied from it. But scholars and some historians are now thinking the opposite is true. They believe the *Epic* is about an earlier story. Many others don't or won't consider the earlier story is the Genesis flood. Remember, they date Genesis to the time of the Babylonian Captivity in 605 BC.

Gilgamesh was handsome and strong. No one could beat him. He was lord over men according to the *Epic*, and he built the walls of Uruk with baked bricks and overlaid the exterior with copper. He went out into the lands around, and the *Epic* says "no son was left to his father" because he took them all.[5] The women too. Before young girls could marry, they had to act like his wife. The people complained Gilgamesh was not a good king. He did not take care of the people like a shepherd would his sheep.

They asked their god for an enemy to come against him, someone who would be equal to him. "Stormy heart for stormy heart," they said. This was Enkidu, a man with long, perhaps brownish blonde hair, and a hairy body. He too was strong and muscular. They were enemies at first. But after Gilgamesh fought Enkidu, they became friends. Later they went on a journey together.

---

[4] J.A. Black, et al. "Gilgamesh and Aga." The Electronic Text Corpus of Sumerian Literature.

[5] N. K. Sanders. "The Epic Of Gilgamesh." Assyrian International News Agency.

Noah

This adventure is called the Forest Journey. Gilgamesh had a dream and decided to go the land of cedars. He said his name had not been inscribed on bricks where famous men lived, the Country of the Living. He wanted to go to this great forest because there was an evil god there. Considering Gilgamesh was not a good person, we can only wonder about what he considered evil.

Enkidu did not want to go at first and warned Gilgamesh against trying to fight the god who never slept and guarded the forest. But Gilgamesh consulted with his people and offered sacrifices to his gods. He asked his mother to give him a sign or word from the gods. Her word was go to the place their god, Shamash, hated. Enkidu was to guard Gilgamesh and allow him to return safely. Lugulbanda was also to guard him. Lugulbanda in this story is Gilgamesh's father in spirit form.

They set off, crossing mountains and finally arrived in the forest. It mentions Lebanon, a place in the Bible known for its cedars. Some think the mountain is Masis in Armenia. Other scholars interpret the Sumerian word *Mashu* to describe the area of Mt. Lebanon and Mt. Hermon.[6]

Gilgamesh used sorcery to give him dreams and guidance. Huwawa, god of the forest, had the face of a lion, and his voice roared like that of a flood. But when this god spoke to him, Gilgamesh fell down as if dead. He killed the god Huwawa. Gilgamesh also killed the god called the Bull of Heaven sent to destroy men and crops.

After his friend Enkidu died, Gilgamesh began thinking about his own death. He realized while some people were dying, there were those who lived extremely long. He wanted to live forever.

Gilgamesh went to visit his relative who lived in a remote place near the mouth of rivers. This man was Utnapishtim. He was ancient and thought to be immortal. The god Enki had commanded Utnapishtim to build a big ship

---

[6] Rivkah Schärf Kluger *The Archetypal Significance of Gilgamesh: A Modern Ancient Hero*. Pg163.

Empire Builders

called the Preserver of Life. On this ship he was to take his family, baby animals and food. Utnapishtim did not like Gilgamesh, but his wife felt sorry for him. He then gave Gilgamesh a plant to make him young. But on the way home a serpent stole the plant, and Gilgamesh gave up the idea of living forever.

Some scholars and Christian historians think Gilgamesh was really Nimrod. George Smith was one of them. Dr. David Livingston was another. Genesis 10:8-12 gives us a history of Nimrod. "And Cush begat Nimrod: he began to be a mighty one in the earth. He was a mighty hunter before the LORD: wherefore it is said, Even as Nimrod the mighty hunter before the LORD." (Genesis 8:9-10) He was the first powerful man after the flood.

The word translated mighty one or powerful is *gibbôwr* (gib-ORE), and it means valiant, warrior, tyrant and champion. *Gibbôwr* is used again before hunter. John Gill (*Gill's Commentary*) said the wording could refer to hunting wild animals. He was a valiant hunter or champion hunter. But Gill pointed out the description is out of place with the next verse. "And the beginning of his kingdom was Babel, and Erech, and Accad, and Calneh, in the land of Shinar." (Genesis 10:10) The word used as hunter is *tsayid* (SIGH-yid). It carries the meaning of chase and take in as to eat. Why is this description given to a man who built a kingdom?

Fausset's Bible Dictionary describes Nimrod as a man who changed the father-son family ruling system of patriarchs. He disrespected fathers. He began taking land and settlements away from those in Assyria to add to his territory. Thus Ham took Shem's and Japheth's cities, violating a tribe based system.

When an animal ignores its instincts, it can become prey. When men turn their spirit from God, they become prey for their adversary, Satan. Nimrod may have started out hunting animals, but it became hunting men and kingdoms. That is why some translations call Nimrod a hunter of men. He was the first tyrant to build a kingdom.

Noah

Nimrod translated into Hebrew means rebellious. According to Dr. David Livingston, the Hebrew is formed from the verb *marad*. It literally becomes The Rebel. Livingston thinks Nimrod may not be his birth name. There are many Hebrew stories about Nimrod, but most do not honor him. One, in Targum Jonathan, says he left the tower in Babel because the people were evil, and God gave him the cities in Assyria. Traditionally, however, he has a bad reputation. In the verse "a mighty hunter before the Lord," some Jewish rabbis translate before as in the sense of opposition to God. We might say, "In His face."

The scholars who connect Nimrod with Gilgamesh see similarities in the two men. Both are described as powerful. Both are considered sinful and in opposition to the God who never sleeps and whose voice is like thunder. Nimrod lived during the time of Noah and witnessed younger generations born with shorter life spans.

Ham had Cush who had Nimrod. Nimrod was born in generation 13. Also in generation 13 is Shem's grandson Shelah. (Shem had Arpachshad who had Shelah.) He was Nimrod's cousin. Shelah was approximately 64 years old when Peleg was born in generation 15. Shelah lived to be 433 years old. We might guess Nimrod lived near to that, but we don't know for sure because the Bible does not say.

One thing Shelah witnessed was the death of Peleg and Nahor, born to generations 15 and 18. Both died before Noah. If they died, there were likely more people dying from those generations. Peleg is the first death recorded after the flood. It may have been news. Noah was still living. So were Shem and Arpachshad. Perhaps Ham, Cush and Japheth too. But people born after them in later generations were living shorter lives. If Shelah lived to see these things, Nimrod probably did too.

When Bible scholars study the *Epic of Gilgamesh* they see nuggets of truth. Gilgamesh, an early king wanted to know Utnapishtim's secret for long life.

Utnapishtim is a Noah-like figure, and it is not outlandish to consider Noah would have chosen to live isolated from the rest of the riff raff. Like near the mouth of two rivers on an island as described in the *Epic*.

The place is named Dilmun, the garden of the sun, in the *Epic*. Many think this is modern Socotra Island off Yemen near the Gulf of Aden. According to *Enmerkar and the Lord of Aratta* the ziggurats were built before Dilmun was settled. The Dilmun civilization was thought to cover what is today Kuwait, Bahrain, Qatar and the eastern portions of Saudi Arabia. The capital is now known to be near the city of Saar in northwestern Bahrain.

Also, in Gilgamesh's story the serpent stole man's ability to live forever on the earth, a story Nimrod would have known about Adam and Eve. Is Nimrod Gilgamesh? No one can say for certain. But there are similarities. What about the god Huwawa? Is he the YHWH (Yahweh) of the Bible? Some interpret Huwawa as another ruler, not a god. We may never know, but Gilgamesh fell down as if he were dead in his presence. That has happened to a few people in the Bible when they encountered heavenly beings. Ezekiel and Daniel did. (Ezekiel 1:28, 3:23, 43:3, 44:4; Daniel 8:17, 10:9) Roman soldiers did. (Matthew 28:4, John 18:6) So did Paul and his cohorts. (Acts 26:14) Gilgamesh saw something or heard something on his Forest Journey.

Mt. Hermon is in the Golan Heights of Israel. The Jordan River begins nearby. It was the home of the nephalim, giants, in the Old Testament. King Solomon called it the Tower of Lebanon. It is where Peter proclaimed Jesus the Messiah in Matthew 16:16 among the old high places of Baal. Many think this is where the Transfiguration of Matthew 17 took place. If this is where Gilgamesh went, the location may be significant.

Gilgamesh also wrote the *Epic* after he returned from his adventure. The purpose of the story was to make him look good, god-like, stronger than ever. Of course he would say he killed God even if it was the God of the Bible whom he encountered. "God is dead," he reported. Like *Time Magazine* October 22, 1965, "We must recognize that the death of God is a historical event: God has died in our time, in our history, in our existence."[7] In this way, Gilgamesh could promote himself and his ideas.

Of course Gilgamesh would pervert Noah's story, if it were Noah he talked to. Gilgamesh wanted to elevate his gods. But he had to invent their accomplishments. He had to bolster their reputation. And Enkidu, if he were a real person was dead. No eyewitness to rat on him. Not that anyone would have dared to, probably.

Gilgamesh was famous in the ancient world. Archaeology has unearthed tablets from Sumer, Babylon, Assyria, Canaan and the Hittite Empire with his name on them. Nimrod and Gilgamesh would have been very early kings. Some scholars connect Sargon the Great, king of Akkad, with Nimrod. Sargon was an empire builder and a violent man. Sargon and Gilgamesh were rebels against God, and Nimrod was a rebel. But Sargon lived later, most likely after Abraham. David Rohl thinks Enmerkar is Nimrod. Perhaps there is someone else we have yet to discover.

In 2003, during the war in Iraq, an important discovery was made in the desert where the Euphrates River once flowed. The BBC and the Assyrian International News Agency reported Uruk and Gilgamesh's tomb had been found by German archaeologists. According to the legends, Gilgamesh was buried in the place the river changed its course. The Iraq War hindered progress at the site, and looting by the locals was a concern. There have been no updates. Someday we may learn more about Gilgamesh. Or Nimrod.

When languages were suddenly changed at the Tower of Babel, there must have been those who were awed by the power of God. But the Bible says Nimrod built cities like Uruk which we know were dedicated to the worship of

---

7 "Theology: The God Is Dead Movement." *Time Magazine.*

false gods. The first was Babel, a city for which the Bible has nothing good to say. Nimrod's type of religion spread through the land. Idols and altars to ancient gods had their beginnings there. The *Keil and Delitzsch Commentary* states Nimrod insisted on turning men from God. It says the destruction of the Tower only made him more determined. Force was the method he used to accomplish his goals.

If a man is known by his fruit, what he produces, then The Rebel and Hunter of Men otherwise known as Nimrod must have been an evil man. Babylon was not a godly city. The book of Revelation (18:2) states Babylon is the place where demons live. All pagan religions have something in common with its theology.

One of Nimrod's cousins was Asshur. But in Genesis 10 we learn Nimrod went to the land of Asshur (Assyria) and built cities there. He may have taken the land by force. Later, Assyria is called the land of Nimrod. Assyria was also a place where idols were worshipped. One of the gods they worshipped was Asshur. Evolutionists think the Bible copied the name, but in reality people began worshipping an ancestor. Assyria too became a violent empire.

Nimrod didn't forget the truth of God. He rejected it. He could have visited Noah, his grandfather Ham or his uncle Shem to talk about God or the flood. Gilgamesh also rebelled against the gods and killed them or stopped their power and message. We may never know for sure if the Gilgamesh story was really about Nimrod. The important thing to remember about the *Epic of Gilgamesh*, is his story is not the real story of Noah. It is not the story that inspired the flood. The flood inspired it, and the *Epic's* purpose was to pervert the truth.

Some believe Nimrod was the man who led the people to build the Tower. The Bible does not say that. It says, "And they said," meaning the people. The word used for them is *bên,* son or children. (Genesis 11:4-5) The ancient legends of Enmerkar and Gilgamesh seem to imply these men experienced the event, but they used the confusion and chaos to benefit themselves and build a kingdom. Nimrod may have done the same. If he were the leader, he must have been very angry God stopped his project. For whatever reason, Nimrod set himself against God to become a powerful leader. And people followed him.

Do you ever think about who influences you? Who we choose to be friends with says a lot about who we are and what we value. 1 Corinthians 15:33 warns us not to be fooled into thinking who we spend our time with doesn't matter. Even if we start out being good and doing good, people of bad character will make us bad.

Evolutionists and unbelievers continue to repeat that the *Epic* and other legends inspired the Genesis flood story. Anne Habermehl said the practice started out by inserting the word probably, and eventually the probably was dropped. Evolutionists hold up their stone tablets and remind us they are older than the Bible. No kidding. The Bible says the same thing. Moses wrote the stories down in Genesis.

But here's the difference: Moses didn't make them up. The content in Genesis is older than their tablets. The stories are facts. Real history. Real science. Real psychology. Real math and physics. There are no myths. God spoke His words for a reason, and He didn't waste His words.

In fact the Bible tells us who wrote their tablets. Archaeologists and historians would have never known what to look for or what they were looking at if it weren't for the Bible. They seem to forget there was no book of the Sumerian King List on coffee tables in modern homes authenticated by archaeology. It is the Bible that is the only documentation which has endured into modern times whole. The Dead Sea Scrolls have proven that.

Nimrod began a movement which thrust man's history into an epic of its own. Great empires followed. The Sumerian, Akkadian, Babylonian, Egyptian,

Hittite, Assyrian, Persian, Greek and Roman Empires are all part of the Bible. The Mitanni, Elamites, Kushites, Medes, Israelites, Philistines, Canaanites and others are involved too.

Again we see Noah's family multiplied and moved from the area of the Armenian Highlands. Some of the people's territories overlapped and grew into new territories. They settled in one area, and some of them left to join people in another region.

Professor Johannes Krause is the Director of the Max Planck Institute for the Science of Human History. He is interested in human evolution and uses DNA from ancient remains to research origins. His studies have found Neanderthals had the same language gene as modern man. In other words he could speak. We've already covered that topic in Chapter 1, but it is interesting he made his discovery using DNA in a search for man's origins.

His other research has traced ancient Europeans to Mesopotamia. We learned that too. From the Bible and elsewhere.

But in 2017 Dr. Krause discovered ancient Egyptians are also descended from people in the Near East. In fact, they have no sub-Saharan African genes, and are closely related to Europeans. The Near East is the Levant part of the Fertile Crescent. This is a blow to the archaic ape man named Adam.

But it supports David Rohl's theory. He used the Bible for inspiration to conclude they came to Egypt out of Mesopotamia. They traveled by boat around the Sinai Peninsula. He points to their god Horus as a form of Ham.

Most important, Krause's research doesn't support evolutional theory stating Egyptians migrated from the jungles of Africa. What happens when DNA research shows all ancient cultures have ancestors from Mesopotamia? Nothing. More elaborate tales will be spun by the never ending creativity of evolution.

One empire not as well known as the Egyptian or Roman is the Hittite Empire. Hittites lived in Turkey and northern Iraq. Their language is considered a source for the oldest known Indo-European languages. There are those who think the Hittites were related to the Hethites of Canaan. The differences in their language may indicate they were not, however. Some linguists, people who study languages, want to call the Hittite language Indo-Hittite. They say it dates from 2,000 BC to 1900 BC. Remember the flood was dated 2348 BC and Peleg was born around 2247 BC? At least the linguists are close to the biblical record.

It may be confusing to understand all the dates we've discussed in our study of Noah. The important thing to know is evolutionists in archaeology are discovering their ideas for ancient man and what he knew and how he lived are wrong. He was smarter and more skilled than they thought. Also, their dating methods have flaws. Archaeology is not perfect science.

Methods used to date ancient artifacts each have their faults. Carbon 14 and radiometric methods depend on the idea that the flow of atoms and decay rates are constant. But variations have been observed. Other problems include contamination of sources. Some experiments have dated recent lava flows older than ancient ones in the Grand Canyon and New Zealand. All we can truly say about dates concerning man's history is they are old, older, not so old and hope there is written history to help us.

An evolutionary timeline uses periods of years. The one used in the Middle East for the "stone age" begins 2 billion years ago. This is the Paleolithic age. It is the section where ape became man and used stone tools, spanning roughly 2 billion BC to 10,000 BC. The following periods are Mesolithic: 10,000-8,000 BC, adding hunter-gatherers, some using rock or clay to make buildings; Neolithic: 8,000-5,000 BC add farming, bone tools, making pottery, better buildings and creating towns; Chalcolithic: 5,000-3,000 BC add using copper.

We've discussed the problems with the chart. The ape/man, gatherer only, has never been found, and recent discoveries place intelligent builders, sculptors, pottery makers, metal workers, writers and farmers in the place of the missing ape.

Facts about ancient people are not confusing if you read the Bible. Let's recap the biblical history of mankind. Before he disobeyed, Adam did not have to hunt or fish or farm. He gathered food from plants and trees to eat. He never had to worry about food, clothes or shelter because God provided it for him. But after Adam disobeyed, he had to leave the garden. Adam had to provide for himself. His life was now filled with toil in pursuit of all the things he needed to live. The gatherer became the farmer...and gatherer.

Noah was also a farmer, before he became a ship builder and after. When Noah's family left the ark, God told them they could eat meat. All of them needed to eat. His children and grandchildren learned how to farm by helping him. They farmed, hunted, fished, gathered wild food, kept goats, sheep, cattle, birds and saved seeds to plant. The locations of the archaeologists' discoveries fit where Noah's children and grandchildren were first and where they traveled after their languages were changed. They began building cities, then empires.

It is that simple. Yet it is fascinating isn't it? Early Babylonian kings like Nabonidus and historians like Herodotus were among the first archaeologists. Ancient men in Europe, China, and the Middle East were interested in the history and lives of more ancient men. It was a hobby to some and to others a way of recording the past.

Historians wrote history. Sometimes they exaggerated to please kings. Sometimes they recorded an event as they understood it, not perhaps as someone else who lived at the time might have described it. Most of the time historians told the truth.

Early archaeologists were adventurers interested in history. Sometimes they collected what they found. Sometimes they sold their artifacts to museums. Many of their discoveries remained mysteries for years.

Soon the adventurers were joined by a group of men more serious in their study of history. They did not want to tell a story to please anyone. They were only interested in what they could uncover. Sir Richard Colt Hoare was one of these men. He excavated at Stonehenge in England in 1798 and 1810. He said, "We speak from facts not theory."[8]

The idea that history and archaeology go together was expressed by an old saying, "Archaeology is the handmaid of history." This means archaeology could prove things historians had recorded.

Archaeology began to be treated seriously in the 1800s and increased in importance in the early 1900s. Today archaeologists use scientific methods to analyze their discoveries. But it is a flawed method as we have learned. History is researched by comparing sources and studying ancient literature and stone or clay tablets. The information is dependable if the source can be trusted.

The Bible is one historical source archaeology has proven to be accurate. Every time someone said a king, town or people group named in the Bible didn't exist, archaeology would discover they did. One example is Sargon, the Assyrian king. His name is mentioned once in the Bible. (Isaiah 20:1) No one ever heard of him or found anything to prove he existed. But in 1842, a French archaeologist found Sargon's name written on the wall in the ruins at Khorsabad, Iraq.

Today there are some archaeologists who refuse to believe the "facts" they find. We have seen this over and over in our study of Noah. Especially if the facts relate to what the Bible has to say about ancient man and ancient history. The Bible is labeled myth where there is no understanding. As if they are the holders of all knowledge. So the humiliation builds because the Bible repeatedly illuminates the limits of their wisdom. Still, they continue to look for evidence of their own notions, like evolution.

---

[8] Richard Colt Hoare. *The Ancient History of Wiltshire*. Page 6.

Empire Builders

Once upon a time, people who did not believe the Bible invented a theory. They said if one could prove the Bible was not accurate about historical things, then one could claim it was not accurate about spiritual things either.

But, the Bible was proven historically accurate over and over again. And, it is still being proven to be accurate. William F. Albright said, "Discovery after discovery has established the accuracy of innumerable details, and has brought increased recognition to the value of the Bible as a source of history."[9]

The problem is getting the people who made up the theory to admit this. Even so, they are hoping the world doesn't notice the truth their theory does reveal. If the Bible is proven historically accurate, it must be accurate about spiritual things like sin and salvation. Instead, all the careful study, all the thousands and thousands of artifacts found have increased unbelief because people refuse to see what is in front of them.

The Bible says, "...the natural man receiveth not the things of the Spirit of God: for they are foolishness unto him: neither can he know them, because they are spiritually discerned." (1Corinthinas 2:14) In the beginning of this book we learned about sense knowledge. The natural man is the flesh man. He learns everything he knows through his senses, the body and the mind.

As empires began, many forgot the revelation of God. They made gods to satisfy their senses, what they could see, what they could hold. By the time of Abraham, during the early dynasty in Ur, idols were a common fixture in Mesopotamia. Abraham's father worshipped idols (Joshua 24:2), probably the god of Ur called Nanna or Sin, the moon god.

But Shem still walked the earth. Kings like Melchizedek worshipped God and were kept safe so they could minister to others, including Abraham. God has always had those who believe in Him. Even when it was only one man named Noah.

---

[9] William F. Albright. *The Archaeology of Palestine.* Page 127

Conclusion

What is the major lesson Noah teaches us, his sons and daughters? Take God's word seriously. When God told him about things he needed to prepare for, things no one had ever witnessed, he listened. Then he acted. He understood what God says happens.

We hope you have been inspired to grab hold of that concept on your journey, and the various discoveries shared have strengthened your confidence in living life boldly in Jesus because the Bible is truth.

Thank you for purchasing *Noah*. If you have enjoyed the read, please leave a review online. You can check out more titles on our website flyingeaglepublications.com or join our email list to receive information on discounts or offers. You can also like our Facebook page to receive updates.

Bibliography

ABC Radio Sydney. "Aboriginal astronomy the star of Dreamtime stories." Wendy Harmer. ABC Radio Sydney. April 4, 2017. Accessed May 15, 2018. http://www.abc.net.au/news/2017-04-05/aboriginal-astronomy-basis-of-dreamtime-stories-stargazing/8413492

Abel, K. "5 Ancient Black Civilizations That Were Not in Africa." Atlanta Black Star. April 16, 201 Accessed July 27, 2018. https://atlantablackstar.com/2014/04/16/5-ancient-black-civilizations-africa/5/

Albright, William F. *The Archaeology of Palestine*, revised edition, Harmondsworth, Middlesex: Pelican Books, 1960. Pages127,128.
Albright, William F. *Recent Discoveries in Bible Lands*. The Biblical Colloquium. New York: Funk & Wagnalls. 1955. Page 25.

Aling Charles. "Cultural Change and the Confusion of Language in Ancient Sumer." Associates for Biblical Research. September 21, 2009. Accessed July 23, 2018. http://www.biblearchaeology.org/post/2009/09/21/Cultural-Change-and-the-Confusion-of-Language-in-Ancient-Sumer.aspx

Al-Rawi, F. N. H. and A. R. George (SOAS, University of London)
"Back to the Cedar Forest: The Beginning and End of Tablet V of the Standard Babylonian Epic of Gilgameš," Journal of Cuneiform Studies 66 (2014), Pages 69–90.

Altein, Yehudah. "The Story of Noah and the Ark in the Bible." Chabad.org Accessed May 22, 2018. https://www.chabad.org/library/article_cdo/aid/246609/jewish/The-Story-of-Noah-and-the-Ark-in-the-Bible.htm

Andrews, Evan. "9 Things You May Not Know About the Ancient Sumerians." History A+E Television Networks. December 16, 2015. Accessed July 24, 2018. https://www.history.com/news/9-things-you-may-not-know-about-the-ancient-sumerians

Answers Magazine editors. "A Glimpse into Life after Babel." *Answers Magazine* Volume 12.3 pg 40 Answers in Genesis. May 1, 2017. Accessed August 18, 2018. https://answersingenesis.org/human-evolution/glimpse-life-after-babel/

Archaeology and Arts contributor. "The Tower of Babel, King Nebuchadnezzar II and the Schøyen Collection Archaeology." Accessed July 17, 2018. https://www.archaeology.wiki/blog/2011/12/29/the-tower-of-babel-king-nebuchadnezzar-ii-and-the-sch%C3%B8yen-collection/

Argubright, John. "Sargon King of Assyria." in *Bible Believer's Archaeology* Vol 3. Accessed July 24, 2018. http://www.biblehistory.net/newsletter/sargon.htm

Ark Encounter editors. "How Big Was Noah's Ark?" Ark Encounter. Accessed March 13, 2018. https://arkencounter.com/noahs-ark/size/

Balter, Michael. "First Farmers Were Also Sailors." *Science Magazine.* June 9, 2014. Accessed July 18, 2018. http://www.sciencemag.org/news/2014/06/first-farmers-were-also-sailors

Benner, Jeff. "Serabit el-Khadim Inscription." Ancient Hebrew Research Center. Accessed May 8, 2018. www.ancient-hebrew.org/inscriptions/104.html
Benner, Jeff. "The Tower of Babel: Fact or Fiction?" Ancient Hebrew Research Center. Accessed February 13, 2018. http://www.ancient-hebrew.org/articles_babel.html

Berke, Jeremy. "More than 100 'uncontacted' tribes exist in total isolation from global society." *Business Insider* Mar. 6, 2018. Accessed May 15, 2018. https://www.businessinsider.com/uncontacted-tribes-where-do-they-live-2016-6

Berkowitz, Adam Eliyahu. "Did Geologists Discover 'Fountains of the Deep' From Genesis Flood?" Breaking Israel News. March 13, 2018. Accessed July 11, 2018. https://www.breakingisraelnews.com/104128/did-geologists-discover-fountains-of-the-deep-from-genesis-flood/
Berkowitz, Adam Eliyahu. "Mummy DNA May Prove Ancient Egyptians Descended From Son of Noah Exactly as Bible Describes." Breaking Israel News. June 22, 2017. Accessed July 27, 2018. https://www.breakingisraelnews.com/90106/dna-study-mummies-indicates-ancient-egyptians-descended-biblical-ham/

Bible History Online contributors. "Sargon II Relief." Bible History Online. https://www.bible-history.com/archaeology/assyria/sargon-II-relief.html
Bible History Online contributors. "Table of Nations." Bible History Online. Accessed July 19, 2018. https://www.bible-history.com/maps/2-table-of-nations.html
Bible History Online contributors. "Ur of the Chaldees." Bible History Online. Accessed July 9, 2018. https://www.bible-history.com/geography/ur_of_chaldees.html

Black, J.A. G. Cunningham, E. Robson, and G. Zólyomi. "Enmerkar and the lord of Aratta: translation" The Electronic Text Corpus of Sumerian Literature. Oxford 1998-2006. Accessed July 12, 2018. http://etcsl.orinst.ox.ac.uk/section1/tr1823.htm
Black, J.A. G. Cunningham, E. Robson, and G. Zólyomi. "Gilgamesh and Aga." The Electronic Text Corpus of Sumerian Literature. Oxford 1998-2006. Accessed July 12, 2018. http://www-etcsl.orient.ox.ac.uk/Oxford 1998-2006.
Black, J.A., G. Cunningham, E. Robson, and G. Zólyomi. "Sumerian King's List." translation The Electronic Text Corpus of Sumerian Literature , Oxford 1998- 2006. Accessed July 28, 2018. (http://www-etcsl.orient.ox.ac.uk/)

Bonner, Walt. "Hebrew may be world's oldest alphabet." Fox News. December 05, 2016. Accessed June 4, 2018. http://www.foxnews.com/science/2016/12/05/hebrew-may-be-worlds-oldest-alphabet.html

Bower, Bruce. "Oldest alphabet identified as Hebrew." *Science News*. November 19, 2016. Accessed June 4, 2018. https://www.sciencenews.org/article/oldest-alphabet-identified-hebrew

Boyd, Steven W. "The Last Week before the Flood Noah on Vacation or Working Harder than Ever?" *Answers Research Journal.* 9 (2016):197–208 https://answersingenesis.org/answers/research-journal/

Boyle, Alan. "African-American's Y chromosome sparks shift in evolutionary timetable." NBC News. March 5, 2013. Accessed July 23, 2018. https://www.nbcnews.com/sciencemain/african-americans-y-chromosome-sparks-shift-evolutionary-timetable-1C8710411

Bradford, Alina. "Carnivores: Facts About Meat Eaters." Live Science. January 22, 2016. Accessed May15, 2018. https://www.livescience.com/53466-carnivore.html

Bridges, Andrew. "Rare Jellyfish Fossils Unearthed in Wisconsin." *Los Angeles Times.* February 17, 2002. Accessed May 17, 2018. http://articles.latimes.com/2002/feb/17/local/me-28479

Britannica, The Editors of Encyclopaedia. "Greek Fire." Encyclopædia Britannica. December 05, 2016. Accessed June 11, 2018. https://www.britannica.com/technology/Greek-fire.
Britannica, The Editors of Encyclopaedia. "Ptolemy IV Philopator Macedonian King Of Egypt." *Encyclopaedia Britannica.* April 11, 2013. *Accessed February 8, 2018.* https://www.britannica.com/biography/Ptolemy-IV-Philopator
Britannica, The Editors of Encyclopaedia. "Sanchuniathon" Encyclopaedia Britannica https://www.britannica.com/biography/Sanchuniathon

BT Library contributors. "Shinar." Biblical Training Library. Accessed July 10, 2018. https://www.biblicaltraining.org/library/shinar
BT Library contributors. "Sumer." Biblical Training Library. Accessed July 10, 2018. https://www.biblicaltraining.org/library/sumer

Callawa, Ewen. "Divided by DNA: The uneasy relationship between archaeology and ancient genomics." *Nature International Journal of Science.* March 28, 2018. Accessed July 16, 2018. https://www.nature.com/articles/d41586-018-03773-6

Carter, Robert W. "Skin colour surprises." *Creation Ministries International* November 23, 2017. https://creation.com/skin-colour-surprises

Cartwright, Mark. "Phoenician Religion." Ancient History Encyclopedia. April 4, 2016. Accessed May 9, 2018. https://www.ancient.eu/Phoenician_Religion/

Chaffey, Tim. "Giants in the Old Testament." *Answers in Depth* Vol. 7. February 22, 2012. Accessed May 9, 2018. https://answersingenesis.org/bible-characters/giants-in-the-old-testament/

Creation Ministries International editors. "When did animals become carnivorous?" Creation.com August 31, 2014. Accessed July 23, 2018. https://creation.com/animal-carnivory-began-at-fall

Creation Studies Institute contributors. "Does The Ancient Sumerian Language Predate The Flood?" Creation Studies Institute. Accessed August 7, 2018. http://www.creationstudies.org/articles/who-is-god/341-ancient-sumerian

Cumberland, Richard. *Sanchoniatho's Phœnician History.* London: W.B. for R.W. Wilkin, 1720. Accessed February 7, 2018. https://archive.org/details/sanchoniathosph00eratgoog

Curry, Andrew. "World's Oldest Temple to Be Restored." *National Geographic.* January 20, 2016. Accessed May 8, 2018. https://news.nationalgeographic.com/2016/01/150120-gobekli-tepe-oldest-monument-turkey-archaeology/

David, Ariel. "400,000-year-old 'School of Rock' Found in Prehistoric Cave in Israel." Haartz. Nov 22, 2017. Accessed February 13, 2018. https://www.haaretz.com/archaeology/MAGAZINE-400-000-year-old-school-of-rock-found-in-prehistoric-cave-in-israel-1.5626671

Davis, Jud. "Noah's World 24 Hours—Plain as Day." *Answers Magazine.* April 1, 2012. Accessed June 4, 2018. https://answersingenesis.org/days-of-creation/24-hours-plain-as-day/

Dundes, Alan. *The Flood Myth.* London, England. University of California Press, Ltd. 1988

Duursma, K.J. "The Tower of Babel account affirmed by linguistics." *Journal of Creation* 16(3):27–31. December 2002. Accessed May 14, 2018. https://creation.com/the-tower-of-babel-account-affirmed-by-linguistics

Edmonds, Margot and Ella E. Clark. *Voices Of The Winds.* New York: Castle Books, 2003.

Espak, Peeter. "Ancient Near Eastern Gods Enki and Ea: Diachronical Analysis of Texts and Images from the Earliest Sources to the Neo-Sumerian Period." Master's Thesis. University of Tartu. 2006.

Faulkner, Danny. "Comments on Ussher's Date of Creation." *Answers Research Journal.* 1 9 (2016):163–169. Accessed July 23, 2018. https://answersingenesis.org/answers/research-journal/

Financial Tribune First Iranian English Economic Daily contributors. "Iran World Heritage Sites: Ziggurat of Chogha Zanbil." Financial Tribune First Iranian English Economic Daily. September 17, 2014. Accessed July 18, 2018. https://financialtribune.com/articles/people-travel/782/iran-world-heritage-sites-ziggurat-of-chogha-zanbil

Food and Agriculture Organization of the United Nations. "Armenia at a Glance." Accessed May 14, 2018. http://www.fao.org/armenia/fao-in-armenia/armenia-at-a-glance/en/

Foroma, Ibo. "Black origins of Mesopotamian civilisation." Rastafarian Perspectives. *The Sunday Mail.* March 26, 2017. Accessed July 9, 2018. http://www.sundaymail.co.zw/black-origins-of-mesopotamian-civilisation/

Frahm, E., E. Jiménez, M. Frazer, and K. Wagensonner. "A Short History of Babylonian and Assyrian Text Commentaries," Cuneiform Commentaries Project 2013–2018. Accessed August 16, 2018. https://ccp.yale.edu/introduction/history-mesopotamian-text-commentaries. DOI: 10079/zcrjdtq

Friedlander, Gerald. *Pirke De Rabbi Eliezer.* London: Kegan, Paul, Trench, Trubner & Co. Ltd. New York: The Bloch Publishing Company. 1916.

Gertoux, Gérard. "A Dating Of The Deluge Is It Attainable?" in *Noah and the Deluge: Chronological, Historical and Archaeological Evidence.* Lulu, 2015. Page 35.

Gertoux, Gérard. "Is The Bible Chronologically And Historically Correct?" in *80 Old Testament Characters of World History: Chronological, Historical and Archaeological Evidence.* Lulu February, 2017. Page 73

Gibbons, Ann. "Meet the frail, small-brained people who first trekked out of Africa." *Science Magazine.* Nov. 22, 2016. Accessed May 15,2018. http://www.sciencemag.org/news/2016/11/meet-frail-small-brained-people-who-first-trekked-out-africa

Gill, John. *Gill's Commentary An Exposition of the Old and New Testaments.* e-Sword.

Grigg, Russell. "Meeting the ancestors: A fascinating observation about the patriarchal lists of early Genesis." *Creation* 25(2):13–15. March 2003. Accessed June 6, 2018. https://creation.com/meeting-the-ancestors

Grigg, Russell. "Who wrote Genesis? Did Moses really write Genesis?" *Creation* 20(4):43–46. September 1998. Accessed June 5, 2018. https://creation.com/did-moses-really-write-genesis

Grimaldi, David and Jes Rust, Michael Engel, et al. "New Trove of Fossils Suggests Global Distribution of Tropical Forest Ecosystems in the Eocene" American Museum of Natural History. Accessed August 8, 2018. https://www.amnh.org/our-research/science-news/2010/new-trove-of-fossils-suggests-global-distribution-of-tropical-forest-ecosystems-in-the-eocene/

Grinnell, George Bird. *Pawnee Hero Stories and Folk-Tales*. Lincoln: University of Nebraska Press, 1961; reprinted from New York: Forest and Stream Publishing Company, 1889.

Guisepi, Robert A. and F. Roy Willis. "Ancient Sumeria." World History Center. Accessed July 16, 2018. http://history-world.org/sumeria.htm

Habermehl, Ann. "Where in the World Is the Tower of Babel?" *Answers Research Journal* 4 (2011):25–53. Accessed May 17, 2018. https://answersingenesis.org/answers/research-journal/

Haughton, Brian. "Gobekli Tepe - the World's First Temple?" Ancient History Encyclopedia. May 4, 2011. Accessed May 14, 2018. https://www.ancient.eu/article/234/gobekli-tepe---the-worlds-first-temple/

Hirsch, Emil G. and Eduard König. "Eber." *Jewish Encyclopedia*. 1906. Accessed May 16, 2018. http://www.jewishencyclopedia.com/articles/5406-eber

Hirst, K. Kris. "Ancient American Civilizations." ThoughtCo. August 7, 2018. Accessed August 18, 2018. https://www.thoughtco.com/top-ancient-american-civilizations-169511

Hirst, K. Kris. "Eridu (Iraq): The Earliest City in Mesopotamia and the World." ThoughtCo. August 2, 2017. Accessed July 10, 2018. https://www.thoughtco.com/eridu-iraq-earliest-city-in-mesopotamia-170802

Hoare, Sir Richard Colt. *The Ancient History of Wiltshire*. Volume 1. Albemarle-Street London: William Miller, 1812. Silent Earth. https://www.silentearth.org/sir-richard-colt-hoare-history-ancient-wiltshire-1812-volume-1/

Hodge, Bodie. "Chapter 28 Was the Dispersion at Babel a Real Event?" in *The New Answers Book 2*. August 19, 2010. Accessed May 15, 2018. https://answersingenesis.org/tower-of-babel/was-the-dispersion-at-babel-a-real-event/

Hodge, Bodie. "Josephus and Genesis Chapter Ten." *Answers in Depth*. Vol. 4 2009. Accessed July 23, 2018. https://answersingenesis.org/genesis/josephus-and-genesis-chapter-ten/

Hodge, Bodie. "How Long Was the Original Cubit?" *Answers Magazine* April 1, 2007. Accessed February 8, 2018. https://answersingenesis.org/noahs-ark/how-long-was-the-original-cubit/

Hoesch, William A. "Out of Ararat?" Institute for Creation Research. September 1, 2006. Accessed May 16, 2018. http://www.icr.org/article/out-ararat/

Holloway, April. "Ten Discoveries of 2014 that Suggest there is Truth to Ancient Myths and Legends." Ancient Origins. December 26, 2014. Accessed May 15, 2018. https://www.ancient-origins.net/news-general/ten-discoveries-2014-suggest-there-truth-ancient-myths-and-legends-002500

Jeanson, Dr. Nathaniel T. "Which Animals Were On the Ark with Noah? Stepping Back in Time" Answers in Genesis. May 28, 2016. Accessed February 7, 2018. https://answersingenesis.org/creation-science/baraminology/which-animals-were-on-the-ark-with-noah/

Kluger, Rivkah Schärf. "The 'Night Sea Journey'," in *The Archetypal Significance of Gilgamesh: A Modern Ancient Hero*. Daimon Verlag, 1991. Page163.

Kramer, Samuel Noah. "The Indus Civilization and Dilmun, the Sumerian Paradise Land." *Expedition Magazine*. 6.3 (1964): n. pag. Expedition Magazine. Penn Museum, 1964 Web. 31 August 2018 <http://www.penn.museum/sites/expedition/?p=740>

Livingston, David. "Who Was Nimrod?" David Livingston. Accessed July 28, 2018. http://davelivingston.com/nimrod.htm

Lopez, Raúl. "The Antediluvian Patriarchs and the Sumerian King List." *Journal of Creation 12, no 3.* December 1, 1998. Pages 347-357 Accessed May 10, 2018. https://answersingenesis.org/bible-history/the-antediluvian-patriarchs-and-the-sumerian-king-list/

Lorey, F. 1997. "The Flood of Noah and the Flood of Gilgamesh." Acts & Facts. 26 (3). Accessed July 13, 2018. http://www.icr.org/article/noah-flood-gilgamesh/

MacIsaac, Tara. "17 Out-of-Place Artifacts Said to Suggest High-Tech Prehistoric Civilizations Existed." Ancient Origins. September 28, 2015. Accessed May 10,2018. www.ancient-origins.net/unexplained-phenomena/17-out-place-artifacts-said-suggest-high-tech-prehistoric-civilizations-020544

Maisels, Charles Keoth. "The Emergence of Civilization: From Hunting and Gathering to Agriculture." in *The Heartland of Cities* .New Fetter Lane, London: Routledge; 1 edition 1993. Page 135.

Mark, Joshua J. "Eridu." Ancient History Encyclopedia. July 20, 2010. Accessed July 16, 2018. https://www.ancient.eu/eridu/
Mark, Joshua J. "Sargon II." Ancient History Encyclopedia. July 3, 2014. Accessed May15, 2018. https://www.ancient.eu/Sargon_II/

McClellan, Matt. "Abraham and the Chronology of Ancient Mesopotamia." *Answers Research Journal.* October 3, 2012. Accessed July 13, 2018. https://answersingenesis.org/bible-timeline/abraham-and-the-chronology-of-ancient-mesopotamia/

McPherson, Brian and Scott McPherson. "Chronology 316: Timeline of Biblical World History." 2012. Acessed February 10, 2018 www.biblestudying.net

Mitchell, Elizabeth. "Evolutionary Language Search Lands at Babel." Answers in Genesis. January 5, 2013. Accessed May 14, 2018. https://answersingenesis.org/tower-of-babel/evolutionary-language-search-lands-at-babel/

Morris, John and Steve Austin. *Footprints in the Ash: The Explosive Story of Mount St. Helens.* Green Forest, Arkansas: Master Books, 2003.

Mosbergen, Dominique. "Oldest-Known Briton 'Cheddar Man' Wasn't Fair-Skinned After All." *Huffington Post*. February 8, 2018. Accessed July 16, 2018. https://www.huffingtonpost.com/entry/cheddar-man-dark-skin-dna-analysis_us_5a7bfffee4b0c6726e0f5874

National Geographic editors. "Mass Extinctions." *National Geographic*. Accessed July 11, 2018. https://www.nationalgeographic.com/science/prehistoric-world/mass-extinction/

Newitz, Annalee. "Hunting for the ancient lost farms of North America." Ars Technica. January 26, 2018. Accessed July 19, 2018. https://arstechnica.com/science/2018/01/hunting-for-the-ancient-lost-farms-of-north-america/

New World Encyclopedia contributors. "Great Flood," New World Encyclopedia. Accessed May 15, 2018. http://www.newworldencyclopedia.org/entry/Great_Flood

Nunn, Warren. "Noah's Ark—water and impact resistant?" *Creation* 36(3):15. July 2014. Accessed February 7, 2018. https://creation.com/noahs-ark-pitch

O'Hair, J. C. "From Adam to Moses." Berean Bible Society. October 26, 2012. Accessed September 13, 2018. https://www.bereanbiblesociety.org/from-adam-to-moses/.

Orr, James, et al. "Riphath" International Standard Bible Encyclopedia (1915) Accessed July 10, 2018. https://www.biblestudytools.com/encyclopedias/isbe/riphath.html

Orr, James, et al. "Shinar." International Standard Bible Encyclopedia (1915) Accessed July 10, 2018. https://www.biblestudytools.com/encyclopedias/isbe/shinar.html

Osanai, Nozomi. "The Background of the Gilgamesh Epic." Answers in Genesis. August 3, 2005. Accessed May 15, 2018. https://answersingenesis.org/the-flood/flood-legends/the-background-of-the-gilgamesh-epic/?sitehist=1517625342002

Osanai, Nozomi. "Chapter 3 A Comparison of Ethics." Answers in Genesis. August 3, 2005. Accessed May 15, 2018. https://answersingenesis.org/the-flood/flood-legends/a-comparison-of-ethics/

Osanai, Nozomi. "A Comparison from Secular Historical Records." Answers in Genesis. August 3, 2005. Accessed May 15, 2018. https://answersingenesis.org/the-flood/flood-legends/a-comparison-from-secular-historical-records/

Osanai, Nozomi. "The Flood Accounts." Answers in Genesis. August 3, 2005. Accessed May 15, 2018. https://answersingenesis.org/the-flood/flood-accounts/

Osanai, Nozomi. "Introduction." Answers in Genesis. August 3, 2005. Accessed May 15, 2018. https://answersingenesis.org/the-flood/flood-legends/flood-gilgamesh-epic/introduction/?sitehist=1517625576108

Osgood, A. J. M. "A Better Model for the Stone Age" *Journal of Creation* 2(1):88–102. April 1986. Accessed July 18, 2018. https://creation.com/a-better-model-for-the-stone-age

Pariona, Amber. "Timeline Of Mass Extinction Events On Earth." Worldatlas. March 5, 2018. Accessed July 11, 2018. https://www.worldatlas.com/articles/the-timeline-of-the-mass-extinction-events-on-earth.html

Parker, Gary. "3.8 How Fast? The Fossil Evidence." Answers in Genesis. March 28, 2016. Accessed May 17, 2018. https://answersingenesis.org/fossils/how-are-fossils-formed/how-fast-fossils-rock-layers/

Pierce, Larry. "In the days of Peleg Ancient documents are consistent with the total accuracy of the Bible's chronology." *Creation* 22(1):46–49. December 1999. Accessed May 16, 2018.   https://creation.com/in-the-days-of-peleg

Pierce, Larry. "The Large Ships of Antiquity." Answers in Genesis. June 1, 2000. Accessed February 8, 2018. https://answersingenesis.org/noahs-ark/the-large-ships-of-antiquity/

Purdom, Georgia and David Menton "Chapter 16 Did People Like Adam and Noah Really Live Over 900 Years of Age?" in *The New Answers Book 2. Answers Magazine*. May 27, 2010. Accessed June 5,2018. https://answersingenesis.org/bible-timeline/genealogy/did-adam-and-noah-really-live-over-900-years/

Sanders, K. *The Epic Of Gilgamesh*. Assyrian International News Agency Books Online. Accessed July 13, 2018. https://archive.org/stream/TheEpicofGilgamesh_201606/eog_djvu.txt

Schuster, Angela M.H. "World's Oldest Ship?" *Archaeology Magazine*. Volume 50 Number 4, July/August 1997. Accessed February 9, 2018. https://archive.archaeology.org/9707/newsbriefs/hayling.html

Science News staff. "Scientists Find Evidence of Small-Scale Farming 23,000 Years Ago in Israel." Science News. July 23, 2015. Accessed July 10, 2018. http://www.sci-news.com/archaeology/science-farming-ohalo-ii-israel-03052.html

Smith, David B. "Çatalhöyük—The First City After Babel?" *Answers Magazine*. December 6, 2015. Accessed July 10, 2018. https://answersingenesis.org/archaeology/%C3%A7atalh%C3%B6y%C3%BCkthe-first-city-after-babel/

Smith, George. *The Chaldean Account of Genesis*. New York: Scribner Armstrong & Co., 1876. https://archive.org/details/chaldeanaccounto00smit

Smith, Sylvia. "Bahrain digs unveil one of oldest civilisations." BBC News. May 21. 2013. Accessed July 9, 2018. https://www.bbc.com/news/science-environment-22596270

Snelling, Andrew A. "Five Mass Extinctions or One Cataclysmic Event?" *Answers Magazine*. February 12, 2017. Accessed July 11,2018. https://answersingenesis.org/geology/catastrophism/five-mass-extinctions-or-one-cataclysmic-event/
Snelling, Andrew A. "Noah's Lost World." *Answers Magazine* April 1, 2014. Accessed May 9, 2018. https://answersingenesis.org/geology/plate-tectonics/noahs-lost-world/
Snelling, Andrew A. "Radiometric Dating: Problems with the Assumptions." *Answers Magazine*. August 4, 2010. Accessed July 18, 2018. https://answersingenesis.org/geology/radiometric-dating/radiometric-dating-problems-with-the-assumptions/

"Some Very Compelling Evidence the Tower of Babel Was Real." from Secrets-Tower of Babel. Smithsonian Channel. Video. Accessed August 20, 2018. https://www.smithsonianmag.com/videos/category/history/some-very-compelling-evidence-the-tower-of-b/

Strickland, Ashley. "Weapons reveal how this 5,300-year-old ice mummy lived -- and died." CNN. June 21, 2018. Accessed August 18, 2018. https://www.cnn.com/2018/06/20/health/otzi-tyrolean-iceman-mummy-new-study/index.html

Tang, Didi. "5,000-year-old primitive writing generates debate in China NBC News. July 11, 2013. Accessed June 4, 2018. https://www.nbcnews.com/science/5-000-year-old-primitive-writing-generates-debate-china-6C10610754

Taylor, Michael. "Letter from Iraq: The Ziggurat Endures." *Archaeology Magazine* Volume 64 Number 2, March/April 2011. Accessed July 19, 2018. https://archive.archaeology.org/1103/letter/american_soldier_ur_iraq.html

Tomkins, Jeffrey P. "Human DNA Variation Linked to Biblical Event Timeline." Institute For Creation Research. July 23, 2012. Accessed May 17, 2018. http://www.icr.org/article/6927/289

Tralfamadore. *Socotra Island The most alien-looking place on Earth.* Atlas Obscura. Accessed July 28, 2018. https://www.atlasobscura.com/places/socotra-island

Truax, E. A. 1991. "Genesis According to the Miao People. Acts & Facts." 20 (4). Accessed July 13, 2018. http://www.icr.org/article/genesis-according-miao-people/.

Ussher, James. *The Annals of the World.* New Leaf Publishing Group, 2003.

Not the same source quoted but an excellent publication:
Ussher, James and Larry Pierce. *Annals of the World: James Ussher's Classic Survey of Ancient World History with CD-ROM.* Green Forest, Arkansas: Master Books, 2003.

von Buseck, Craig. "What did Noah's Ark Look Like?" CBN. Accessed February 8, 2018. http://www1.cbn.com/biblestudy/what-did-noah%27s-ark-look-like%3F

Walton, John. "Is there Archaeological Evidence for the Tower of Babel?" Bible Archaeology. May10, 2008. Accessed July 17, 2018. http://www.biblearchaeology.org/post/2008/05/Is-there-Archaeological-Evidence-for-the-Tower-of-Babel.aspx#Article

Wang, Amy B. "Divers to scour lake for Emperor Caligula's 2,000-year-old pleasure ship." *Washington Post.* April 4, 2017. Accessed March 9, 2018. https://www.washingtonpost.com/news/worldviews/wp/2017/04/04/divers-to-scour-lake-for-emperor-caligulas-2000-year-old-pleasure-ship/?noredirect=on&utm_term=.e0630f4da052

Weisberger, Mindy. "Earth's First Animals Sparked Global Warming, Too." Live Science. July 2, 2018. Accessed August 8, 2018. https://www.livescience.com/62972-first-life-launched-global-warming.html

Weisberger, Mindy. "Fossilized Tropical Forest Found — in Arctic Norway." Live Science. November 20, 2015. Accessed August 8, 2018. https://www.livescience.com/52868-fossil-forests-norway.html

White, Laurie J. *King Alfred's English*. Covington, Georgia: The Shorter Word Press, 2009.

Whitney, Craig R. "Jeanne Calment, World's Elder, Dies at 122." *New York Times*. August 5, 1997. Accessed May 8, 2018. https://www.nytimes.com/1997/08/05/world/jeanne-calment-world-s-elder-dies-at-122.html

Encyclopedias are a good place to begin research and follow leads. Some entries we used and others are for your convenience.

Wikipedia contributors. "Cretaceous–Paleogene extinction event." Wikipedia, The Free Encyclopedia. Accessed July 12, 2018. https://en.wikipedia.org/wiki/Cretaceous%E2%80%93Paleogene_extinction_event

Wikipedia contributors. "Eridu," Wikipedia, The Free Encyclopedia. Accessed July 12, 2018. https://en.wikipedia.org/wiki/Eridu

Wikipedia contributors. "Etemenanki." Wikipedia, The Free Encyclopedia. Accessed July 19, 2018. https://en.wikipedia.org/wiki/Etemenanki

Wikipedia contributors. "Halaf Culture." Wikipedia, The Free Encyclopedia. Accessed July 9, 2018. https://en.wikipedia.org/wiki/Halaf_culture

Wikipedia contributors. "Huwawa." Wikipedia, The Free Encyclopedia. Accessed August 7, 2018. Huwawa https://en.wikipedia.org/wiki/HumbabaWikipedia contributors, "Ötzi," Wikipedia, The Free Encyclopedia, https://en.wikipedia.org/w/index.php?title=%C3%96tzi&oldid=855204339 (accessed August 18, 2018).

Wikipedia contributors. "Serabit el-Khadim." Wiki Visually. Accessed September 13, 2018. https://wikivisually.com/wiki/Serabit_el-Khadim

Wikipedia contributors. "Shipbuilding." Wikipedia, The Free Encyclopedia. June 30, 2018. Accessed August 9, 2018. https://en.wikipedia.org/wiki/Shipbuilding

Wikipedia contributors. "Sinites Creation." Wiki. Accessed May 15, 2018. http://creationwiki.org/Sinites

Wikipedia contributors. "Tudiya." Wikipedia, The Free Encyclopedia, Accessed July

8, 2018. https://en.wikipedia.org/w/index.php?title=Tudiya&oldid=823813682 (accessed August 24, 2018).
Wikipedia contributors. "Ubaid Period" Wikipedia, The Free Encyclopedia. Accessed July 9, 2018. https://en.wikipedia.org/wiki/Ubaid_period
Wikipedia contributors. "Ussher chronology," Wikipedia, The Free Encyclopedia. Accessed May 9, 2018. https://en.wikipedia.org/w/index php?title=Ussher_chronology&oldid=859351165
Wikipedia contributors. "Wyoming (schooner)," Wikipedia, The Free Encyclopedia. June 13, 2018. Accessed August 9, 2018. https://en.wikipedia.org/wiki/Wyoming_(schooner)

Wilson, Clifford. "Genesis and the Lost Tablets." Answers in Genesis. December 1, 1994. Accessed July10, 2018. https://answersingenesis.org/genesis/genesis-and-the-lost-tablets/

Wood, Bryant. "Digging Past the Doubts." *Answers Magazine*. December 31, 2017. Accessed July 23, 2018. https://answersingenesis.org/archaeology/digging-past-doubts/
Wood, Bryant G. "Great Discoveries in Biblical Archaeology: The Nuzi Tablets." Associates For Biblical Research. February 27, 2006. Accessed May 8,2018.http://www.biblearchaeology.org/post/2006/02/27/Great-Discoveries-in-Biblical-Archaeology-The-Nuzi-Tablets.aspx#Article

Wright, David. "Timeline for the Flood." Answers in Genesis. March 9, 2012. Accessed August 16, 2018. https://answersingenesis.org/bible-timeline/timeline-for-the-flood/

Zachos, Elaina. "Antarctica Was Once Covered in Forests. We Just Found One That Fossilized." *National Geographic*. November 15, 2017. Accessed May 9, 2018. https://news.nationalgeographic.com/2017/11/ancient-fossil-forest-found-antarctica-gondwana-spd/

Zimmer, Carl. "How the First Farmers Changed History." *The New York Times* Oct. 17, 2016. Accessed July 18, 2018. https://www.nytimes.com/2016/10/18/science/ancient-farmers-archaeology-dna.html

www.ingramcontent.com/pod-product-compliance
Lightning Source LLC
Chambersburg PA
CBHW071211070526
44584CB00019B/3000